Praise for

FIRST GEN

"FIRST GEN is a gift to all of us—the children of immigrants who have longed to read a story like ours in books. With vulnerability and transparency, Campoverdi gives us special access to so many setbacks, triumphs, and hard-won lessons as a First and Only. Every Latina hoping to end cycles of generational trauma must read this immediately."

—Erika Sánchez, *New York Times* bestselling author of *I Am Not Your Perfect Mexican Daughter*

"FIRST GEN is a luminous achievement, one of the most moving debuts in memory...Campoverdi transforms the furies, hypocrisies, and disappointments of the American Dream into a survivor's song of surpassing poignancy... this is literary love medicine, a book you will not soon forget."

—Junot Díaz, Pulitzer Prize–winning author of *New York Times* bestsellers *The Brief Wondrous Life of Oscar Wao* and *This Is How You Lose Her*

"Intimate and unflinching, FIRST GEN reveals the very real human and emotional costs to living the 'American Dream.' Alejandra Campoverdi shines a guiding light for fellow 'First and Onlys' who struggle to overcome systemic barriers while detangling generational trauma. No discussion of America's supposed meritocracy is complete without consideration of this powerful book."

—Qian Julie Wang, *New York Times* bestselling
author of *Beautiful Country: A Memoir
of an Undocumented Childhood*

"I wish this book existed when I was a first-generation student navigating the alienating world of academia and the mostly white workplaces thereafter. Campoverdi's writing is honest, healing, and empowering. FIRST GEN has made me feel seen and less alone."

—Javier Zamora, *New York Times*
bestselling author of *Solito*

"A profoundly moving story of how one woman grew to appreciate that the painful challenges and self-doubt inherent in being the 'First and Only' were also the source of her extraordinary superpowers. FIRST GEN will inspire countless readers to follow in the path she blazed."

—Valerie Jarrett, former senior advisor to
President Barack Obama and *New York Times*
bestselling author of *Finding My Voice*

"Alejandra is the definitive voice for first-generation young people who maintain their heritage while achieving their ambitions." —Norma Kamali, fashion icon and designer

"FIRST GEN captures the emotional and physical agility required to break generational glass ceilings. Alejandra's captivating memoir reminds us to be bold and brave on race relations, be it in the boardroom or the Oval Office."

—Mellody Hobson, co-CEO
and president of Ariel Investments

"This is a beautiful and powerful book. But, more than anything, it is a truthful one. Campoverdi's life is, in a way, a reflection of everybody's dream in America. She could have told us about all she has achieved—and then suggest that, if she did it, you can, too. Instead, courageously, she tells us how difficult it was: that there is a price to be paid when you are the 'First and Only.'"

—Jorge Ramos, Emmy Award–winning
senior anchor of Univision News and
bestselling author of *The Latino Wave*

"I felt like I found home when I read Alejandra Campoverdi's book. FIRST GEN was written for the person who is looking for connection, understanding, and inspiration. I laughed, I cried, and I felt understood. Being a 'First and Only' can often be isolating, but reading this book affirmed that we are not alone on this journey. Let this book be a calling to all of us who have been the 'First and Only' in the room, at the table, in the class, and at the podium, to come together to form the community that we are often missing but so badly need."

—Mónica Ramírez, activist and founder of
Justice for Migrant Women

"So much resonates in FIRST GEN—from the conflict of achieving the impossible as a 'first' in your family while constantly being pulled back into the drama of dysfunction, to the paradox of having magical breakthroughs on the worst days of your life. Every young person should read this book to understand how to fulfill their dreams while cleaning up generational baggage, to ultimately heal and finally find their true selves."

—Nely Galán, *New York Times* bestselling author of *Self Made: Becoming Empowered, Self-Reliant, and Rich in Every Way*

"FIRST GEN lays out the challenges and contradictions of being a 'First and Only'—may others walking a similar path find hope and inspiration in her story."

—Cecilia Muñoz, former director of the White House Domestic Policy Council and author of *More Than Ready: Be Strong and Be You... and Other Lessons for Women of Color on the Rise*

"Alejandra Campoverdi, with piercing insight and unflinching candor, has written a book for our times—capturing the American Dream as experienced by immigrants and their children who are remaking America. Her story may be one-of-a-kind, but the lessons she learned and imparts are universal."

—Jose Antonio Vargas, Pulitzer Prize–winning journalist and author of national bestseller *Dear America: Notes of an Undocumented Citizen*

FIRST GEN

FIRST GEN

A Memoir

ALEJANDRA CAMPOVERDI

GRAND
CENTRAL

NEW YORK BOSTON

Grand Central Publishing
Hachette Book Group
1290 Avenue of the Americas, New York, NY 10104
grandcentralpublishing.com
twitter.com/grandcentralpub

First Edition: September 2023

Grand Central Publishing is a division of Hachette Book Group, Inc. The Grand Central Publishing name and logo is a trademark of Hachette Book Group, Inc.

The publisher is not responsible for websites (or their content) that are not owned by the publisher.

The Hachette Speakers Bureau provides a wide range of authors for speaking events. To find out more, go to hachettespeakersbureau.com or email HachetteSpeakers@hbgusa.com.

Grand Central Publishing books may be purchased in bulk for business, educational, or promotional use. For information, please contact your local bookseller or the Hachette Book Group Special Markets Department at special.markets@hbgusa.com.

Library of Congress Cataloging-in-Publication Data
Names: Campoverdi, Alejandra, author.
Title: First gen : a memoir / Alejandra Campoverdi.
Description: First edition. | New York : Grand Central Publishing, 2023. | Includes bibliographical references.
Identifiers: LCCN 2023016024 | ISBN 9781538757185 (hardcover) | ISBN 9781538757208 (ebook)
Subjects: LCSH: Campoverdi, Alejandra. | Mexican American women—Biography | Children of immigrants—United States—Biography. | United States. White House Communications Office—Officials and Employees—Biography | Breast—Cancer—Genetic aspects.
Classification: LCC E184.M5 C354 2023 | DDC 305.48/86872073092 [B]—dc23/eng/20230425
LC record available at https://lccn.loc.gov/2023016024

ISBNs: 9781538757185 (hardcover), 9781538757208 (ebook)

Printed in the United States of America

LSC-C

Printing 1, 2023

For the First and Onlys:

*You have been assigned this mountain
to show others it can be moved.*

And for Abi.

CONTENTS

aka Playlist

PROLOGUE: The Promise   1

1.   Fast Car   9

2.   Born on the Bayou   31

3.   *Amor Eterno*   52

4.   Keep Their Heads Ringin'   85

5.   Crash Into Me   113

6.   On the Bound   136

7.   How to Save a Life   164

8.   Everlong   202

9.   *La Trenza*   221

AUTHOR'S NOTE: It's Only Love
That Gets You Through   257

Acknowledgments   271

We will forever be known by the tracks we leave.

—*Dakota proverb*

PROLOGUE

THE PROMISE

I'M GONNA KEEP *it real with you.*

This was the unspoken promise I made to an auditorium full of students at Harvard University's 2016 *Latinx Graduation.* As I approached the podium at my alma mater, I had planned to give remarks of the I-did-it-so-you-can-too variety. But as I stared out at hundreds of earnest faces in identical black gowns, many of them with PRODUCTO DE INMIGRANTES stenciled in white letters across the top of their caps, something about that narrative suddenly felt unfair and incomplete. My gut told me that the moment called for something more truthful. If anything, out of respect. These weren't just any students, after all. They were cycle breakers.

These young people had just white-knuckled their way through school guided solely by the *possibility* of a better life than their parents'. They personified single-minded tenacity and blind faith in the American Dream. And yet, having stood in their shoes over a decade earlier, I knew that many of the unique struggles they'd faced had likely not been validated. They might've even been glossed over or minimized as worthy sacrifices for a greater cause. I was also well aware of the tough realities that were crouching in the wings as these graduates launched themselves into their lives and careers. They hung in the air between us like unidentified mutual ancestors. How could my words of encouragement be helpful to them if I didn't point out the ghosts?

After all, it's not easy to be what I refer to as a *First and Only*—those of us who are the "first generation" or the "only" person in our family, community, or social demographic group to cross a threshold. Some of us are first-generation Americans, first-generation college students, first-generation professionals. Or we're the only person of color, woman, or LGBTQ+ person at the table or in the room. The specific borders we breach are different, but what unites us is a shared familiarity with a particular set of experiences, challenges, and expectations that come with the territory. What I call the *Trailblazer Toll.*

My life to date has been a balancing act on a razor's edge of paradox. In heels. I've been a child on welfare, a White House aide to President Barack Obama, a gang member's girlfriend, and a candidate for the United States Congress. I've ridden on Air Force One and in G-rides. I've been featured in *Maxim magazine* and had a double mastectomy. I recognize how incredibly fortunate I am to have had access to these opportunities—educational, professional, and health-related. And I am grateful for the added perspective and empathy that come with living a life of contradictory extremes. It is a beautiful thing to be a First and Only, the one who disrupts deep-rooted generational patterns to become our ancestors' wildest dreams. *And* it also comes at a price.

To be a First and Only in America is a delicate balance of surviving where you come from while acting like you belong where you're going. Success in the former does not make the latter any easier. In fact, the more effective you are at surviving, the larger the experience gap there is to bridge. But in reality, First and Onlys aren't crossing a bridge at all. We *are* the bridge—painstakingly stretched from where we come from to where we hope to arrive.

The Trailblazer Toll is the *emotional* cost of social and economic mobility. It's the tax we pay to become the proverbial bridge. I conceived of the phrase because up until now, I've seen surprisingly little about the comprehensive emotional experiences of First and Onlys. Some aspects receive a lot of attention while others are rarely publicly acknowledged, despite being widespread, normal, and even expected. And therein lies the problem. Shifting a paradigm is isolating and terrifying work, and we rarely talk about that part. We focus on the victory lap instead.

It would have been easy, standing at the podium that day at Harvard, to share the glossy version of my life, neatly packaged into six words: from welfare to the White House. But using such an oversimplified shorthand would have been incomplete at best, and misleading at worst—and all too often we're conditioned to do just that. To be so grateful for our opportunities and so protective of our fragile new status that we leave no room for questions, doubts, or our own humanity. But it's unreasonable to create the expectation that any of us can navigate social mobility unscathed.

Certainly, the circumstances of being a First and Only vary, defy simple categorization, and evolve over time.

And the eight components of the Trailblazer Toll that I identify in the pages that follow—drawn from terms and ideas from psychology, sociology, and my own personal experiences—are by no means meant to be exhaustive. Yet by exploring pervasive themes I've seen come up repeatedly in the lives of First and Onlys, I hope to ignite a conversation that is long overdue. My guess is that many of us have at some point come up against one or more of these dynamics:

- The bearing of emotional and behavioral patterns passed down by our ancestors—our *Invisible Inheritances*
- The tendency of First and Onlys to take on the role of an adult—serving as the family translator, doctor go-between, form filler, dictionary, or psychologist—becoming a *Parentified Child* along the way
- The exhaustion of engaging in a *Bicultural Balancing Act*, navigating different cultures, ethnicities, social classes, and communities to become all things to all people
- The unpredictability of our access to opportunity and social hierarchy, which can feel like a game of *Chutes and Social Ladders*
- The isolation of our *Lonely Hustle*, as the chasm between the experiences we share with our family and loved ones becomes wider and our relentless drive to advance becomes less relatable

- The fear that comes with taking financial and career risks with no safety net, akin to *Blindfolded Cliff Jumping*
- The inadequacy we may feel penetrating rooms, workplaces, and systems that have traditionally excluded us, and how these same systems actively reinforce our perceived inferiority regardless of our confidence, leading us to experience *Impostor Syndrome Plus*
- The responsibility to prove that our family's sacrifices were worth it, as well as the self-consciousness of having more financial security than our loved ones, which can lead to *Breakaway Guilt*

These were just some of my emotional reference points when I spoke at Harvard that day.

After the ceremony, students lined up to share their personal stories, many of them with tears in their eyes. I recognized the pain alongside the pride on their faces, because I looked the same at my own graduation. Before that moment, I hadn't realized the extent to which the conflicting emotions I'd felt were actually a prevalent phenomenon. How common it is that those who smash through glass ceilings are then left to clean up the shards on their own.

So then why are we still sold a one-dimensional narrative of what it takes to achieve the American Dream? All the way back to elementary school, we learn about groundbreakers and their rags-to-riches ascents that shatter any limitation. Read the profiles of First and Onlys at the highest levels of government, entertainment, sports, or business, and you will undoubtedly encounter seemingly linear narratives of defying the odds. It's one of the reasons I used to think that I, too, had to be perfect in order to be successful, or even worthy. But I have plenty of scars; I have made many missteps. And pretending I don't doesn't serve me or anyone coming up after me.

Beating the odds is already hard enough: We live in a time of rising income inequality and declining social mobility. There is only a 7.5 percent probability that a child born to parents in the bottom fifth of the income distribution will reach the top fifth. How do we change this? We can start by arming ourselves with the truth. Not a rose-colored Disneyland version of social mobility, but the lived reality that many of us face. How else are we to know that we are not alone, that we are not broken, and that our shared experiences are to be expected? Being seen is a powerful gift, and First and Onlys deserve every fighting chance we can get.

In my own ascent from the bottom 5 percent of Latina earners to the top 5 percent, one thing has become crystal clear: Pain and poverty may travel through generations, but owning one's entire journey can be a radical act of healing. It's what compelled me to examine my own experiences—as a Mexican American woman raised by a single mother in Los Angeles—through new eyes. I retraced past versions of myself and followed their steps like a road map, stopping at pivotal forks along the way. In the process, I discovered that the story of my life—our lives—can't be told neatly in a résumé or with bullet points. And that's the intention of this book: not to center the tidy bullet points but to shine a light on the spaces *between* them.

Which is why my promise to you now is the same as it was to Harvard's class of 2016: I'm gonna keep it real with you. Because I'm committed to correcting the sugarcoated, stereotypical narrative about social mobility and the American Dream. Because I believe that by revealing our wounds to one another, we are all a little more free and a little less alone. And because the first step on any emotional journey is to own the truth. To reclaim the parts of ourselves we sacrificed in order to survive.

Identifying the emotional scar tissue of being a First and Only is not meant to be discouraging; on the contrary, it is essential. Because we can't heal from that which we can't name. It's perhaps our best hope to ensure that we aren't set up for a life lived with outward success but emotional isolation. We can and must hold space for it all. Pain alongside pride. Trauma next to hope. Guilt and success.

To my fellow First and Onlys, we have blazed trails and broken ground for countless others throughout our lives. It's now our time…to heal.

CHAPTER ONE

FAST CAR

WHEN I WAS four, I imagined I was Cinderella. Poor, yet only temporarily. Unknown, yet soon to be discovered. I'd slip into this fantasy whenever my grandmother Abi and I would sweep leaves off the sidewalk in front of our drab apartment building. It gave purpose to every pointless stroke of my broom.

I spent many afternoons on that public sidewalk. I'd shadow Abi (short for *abuelita*) down the stairs from our second-floor apartment, mirroring every move her creased hands made, as fast cars whizzed by and the California sun warmed our necks. We each had a broom—the cheap kind with wooden handles and plastic bristles that you can find at any local drugstore. Only mine was pint-sized and pink. I didn't realize until many years later that this was considered a "You know you're Mexican American when…" kind of thing to do, like blasting Juan Gabriel's music, celebrating Christmas on December 24, or preferring pan dulce to donuts.

We lived in a dingy beige building along a heavily trafficked boulevard on the border of Santa Monica and

Venice, nestled against a car wash and a parking lot. But we were devoted to that sidewalk as if we owned it. Abi had extreme pride of place. She kept our home impeccably, not fazed by the fact that seven of us were crammed into a three-bedroom apartment. What could be better than having her husband, four of her six adult children, and me, her only grandchild, all under the same (albeit small) roof?

Barely standing five foot four, with cropped white hair, warm eyes, and a pudgy body that I affectionately called "my pillow," Abi took her role as family matriarch seriously. She could solve any problem with her daily prayers to *la Virgen*, her handmade flour tortillas, or a bowl of her famous chicken soup. And she lived to help—her family especially, but really anyone who was weak or vulnerable. The homeless man who stood in front of my elementary school received a thermos of coffee every morning. Once, in the middle of the night, hearing a woman scream outside her window, Abi grabbed her broom and ran out the door without hesitation. She chased the man who was assaulting our neighbor down the block in her nightgown, waving the broom in the air like a sword.

I can still see her steeping tea for my grandfather, making sure it reached the ideal saturation point before transferring the depleted tea bag to her own cup of hot water. This was a woman who had seriously considered becoming a nun and would've probably led a convent, had she not dreamed of having children. She brought grace and order everywhere she went. Too bad the two large leafy trees that flanked our front door never cooperated.

Despite our best efforts to regularly sweep dry leaves

and twigs into neat piles, we'd wake up the next day to a freshly blanketed sidewalk. We never made any lasting progress—and it felt that way inside our home too. There never seemed to be enough money, food, or time to go around—no matter how hard anyone worked. To distract myself from the leaves and our lives, I'd escape into a fantasy world all of my own.

I may have been just a shy kid in a bathrobe, but while sweeping the gum-laden sidewalk with Abi, I was a Disney princess waiting for her glass slipper. When I was Cinderella, I didn't mind sweeping the sidewalk. I'd grip the pink handle tighter; my broom would move faster.

"Great job," Abi would say, looking over at my freshly swept gray cement squares. "Now do this side."

I was happy to. Working hard had always been a part of the fairy tale; it was how I'd earn my destiny. One day, I'd be a part of something that truly mattered in the world, and then I, too, would matter. I just had to struggle a bit longer to get there, that's all. Sweep a little harder. One day, I'd walk into the Grand Ball, just like Cinderella, and become the person I was always meant to be.

———

Twenty-five years later, I finally made it to that ball, in a dress Walt Disney himself would've approved of. I stood at the entrance of a gilded neoclassical auditorium in the heart of our nation's capital wearing a custom-designed gown with thirty yards of black taffeta ruffles and pleats that spilled onto the floor like a waterfall. The last time I'd worn a dress halfway that nice was to my junior prom, but my mom took that one back to Nordstrom the very next day (tags expertly reattached). Now, surrounded by gold-leaf-adorned columns and smiling so hard my cheeks hurt, the reality was a million times better than any childhood fantasy. I was attending President Obama's inaugural ball.

I looked around the well-heeled crowd and thought, *I made it. I'm finally here.* The very next morning, I'd be starting my new job in the West Wing of the White House, working for a president who had just made history after an unprecedented campaign that I had been a part of. What's more, I'd be the special assistant to the first Black woman to ever serve as White House deputy chief of staff for policy. I spent the evening mingling around CNN anchors, members of Congress, and Hollywood stars, while holding a sleek champagne flute and pinching myself. In a far corner of the internet, there's even a random photo of me next to Google's Larry Page. I was twenty-nine years old.

For several reasons, I was probably the least likely person in the room to be at the ball. And that made it all the more special. Five years earlier, I was working as a waitress, making minimum wage. Two years after that, I had taken out student loans in the six figures for graduate school. And over the previous year, I had racked up five figures of credit card debt to pay my living expenses so I could work on the Obama campaign. But now I would finally have an opportunity to act toward meaningful change at the highest level and to champion my community in the process. We'd have a seat at the most powerful table.

It was everything I dreamed I could do, and more than I ever dreamed I could be.

Despite the glamour of the night and getting only four hours of sleep, I could not wait for my first day of work. Butterflies woke me up well before my alarm went off. As I stood in front of the bathroom mirror, getting ready, I thought about all the ways that my life was about to change. After years of being underestimated, I felt like I was stepping into my personal power—as a woman and as a professional. Smoothing my black blazer and pencil skirt, I realized that underneath my excitement there was also a sense of relief. From this point on, it was likely that I'd have the kind of career that could support my family if and when anyone fell on bad times. It was a goal that I'd set for myself since I was a child.

The walk to the White House was a straight shot down 16th Street NW, and with each step, my nerves grew. I'd been warned that working in the White House was like drinking from a fire hose—a frenetic pace, sixteen-hour days, crushing stress, and little to no sleep. I tried to reassure myself that I was used to a brutal grind, having worked nonstop since I was in my early teens. But nothing could've prepared me for what I was about to experience. Not the campaign, not even Harvard.

I reported to the Eisenhower Executive Office Building before 8 a.m. for orientation and to receive my work badge. It's hard to imagine a building as awe-inspiring as the White House itself, yet the EEOB stood next door with a grandeur all its own. Built in the late 1880s, the building holds over 550 rooms on ten acres of ornately tiled floors. It's where the majority of White House staff work, given how little office space there is inside the actual White House.

I was handed a navy blue badge with a white W on it—something of a coveted status symbol, but I wasn't aware of that yet. I hadn't come up on campaigns or previously worked on Capitol Hill, like many of my new colleagues. The 2008 presidential campaign had been my very first job in politics, driven solely by my belief in then senator Obama. Before orientation day, I had seen the White House only once, at a distance, through a tall black metal gate.

As I walked through the grounds to find my office, each moment was more surreal than the last. My first stop was a Secret Service checkpoint at the entrance to the lower West Wing. A uniformed man with a buzz cut looked me up and down as I tried my best to not seem suspicious.

"Badge?" he said, with a hint of annoyance that I wasn't wearing one.

"Oh, yes. Sorry." I fumbled through the stack of folders in my arms for the lanyard I'd just been given.

"You need to keep that around your neck at all times, ma'am."

"I will. Sorry," I responded, pulling the badge over my head with one hand and resting it faceup.

When he nodded for me to walk through, I stood there dumbfounded for a few seconds. That was it? I was in?

I entered the West Wing and walked up to the lobby, passing the Roosevelt Room and FDR's portrait staring back at me. I turned the corner and stopped in my tracks in front of a broad doorway that revealed a full view of… the Oval Office. Just ahead of me, at twelve o'clock, was the historic Resolute Desk—empty, but imposing all the same. I had been told that the air was different in the Oval, but I wouldn't know. I was holding my breath.

Past the Oval was a passageway that led to six offices, including those of the chief of staff, a senior advisor to the president, and the vice president. It was a dim, narrow hall with no windows, but this was prime real estate because of its location. You can imagine my shock when this is where I was told I'd sit—ten steps from the Oval Office.

My boss, Mona, was already at her desk when I walked in. I overheard her discussing the most recent job growth numbers on the phone as I passed by, noticing her smart suit and heels. Mona was who I aspired to be—effortlessly polished and brilliant. I immediately promised myself that she'd never beat me to the office again. I would make sure to be in my seat when she arrived and still be sitting there when she left for the day. And I would get to know everything about her. That was the loose job description of a White House special assistant: Be one step ahead of all of your principal's needs. From meetings to briefing materials to the toppings she liked on her oatmeal (brown sugar and raisins).

I settled into my desk, ready to work around the clock and validate her decision to hire me. We had met only days before, in the flurry of hiring right before Inauguration Day. After waiting around DC for a month, I'd been interviewed and offered the position all at once, and I was nervous about living up to her expectations. I spent my first day trying to anticipate the wishes of a stranger, as well as figuring out how the secure phones worked, where we could find some food (the White House Mess), and meeting my new colleagues.

The West Wing housed only a few hundred staff in mostly two cohorts—the bold-faced names you read about in the paper and the young aides who were their assistants, fresh off the campaign and convinced we would change the world. We were all onboarding at the same time, leaving us little room to get to know each other, but I figured there would be plenty of opportunities for that as we settled into the coming weeks and months.

Watching my peers mill around gathering supplies and setting up their secure computers, I couldn't believe how lucky I was that these talented young people would soon be my friends. Everyone seemed so confident and accomplished. And I wasn't the only one fascinated by them. *Politico* was reporting on the comings and goings of White House staffers like it was *DeuxMoi*.

By the time my boss went home that first day and I had quadruple-checked that her briefing materials for the next day were prepped and on her desk, the sky had turned pitch-black. I left through the West Wing lobby's double doors and took a dark path across the North Lawn to Pennsylvania Avenue. When I reached the black metal fence, something told me to turn around. Bathed in bright white light under the moon, the White House was breathtaking.

Remember this moment, I said to myself. *Remember how you feel right this very moment.*

Taking stock of every road that had led to this

instant, I thought of the arc of my family's story. My great-grandmother's factory job as a single mother in Mexico. My grandmother's struggle to raise six kids in Mexico, mostly alone and broke. My mother's first job in the US, making car mats in Compton. And now, I was working in the White House. Generations' worth of Firsts. Generations' worth of Onlys. I would be the one to make everyone's sacrifices worth it.

A picture-perfect story of the American Dream, right? Not exactly.

Four days later, it all came crashing down.

My life is over. That was the thought running in a loop through my mind as I careened into hyperventilating panic. I finally had everything. Career, stability, and, most of all, respectability. The last part may not sound all that significant, but to a First and Only who had never felt like she fully belonged in the spaces she occupied, it was the brass ring of social mobility. Class and belonging. And I had it all. For four days.

It was late at night, and I had been lying in bed scrolling through my phone when a Google Alert appeared at the top of my inbox. During White House orientation, it was suggested that staffers create a Google Alert for our names so that we'd know any time we were mentioned in the media and there would be no surprises. Rumor had it that the White House also created Google Alerts for our names to keep tabs on us. I hadn't expected to see my name in the press at all, let alone during the wall-to-wall national news coverage of the administration's first week. And then I read the words in the email subject line:

WHITE HOUSE'S *MAXIM* BABE

I bolted upright in the dark and gasped. Clicking through the link, I saw her. Early-twenties me leaning awkwardly against a wall, wearing a black corset, with the worst haircut/color I've had in my life. Views of the story were in the hundreds of thousands and rapidly climbing.

Babe.

I winced reading the word. This couldn't be happening. Not now. Not in front of all of my new colleagues. I quickly read the article, each line cutting a little deeper.

There were photos of me in *Maxim* juxtaposed right next to photos of me in a gown at the inaugural ball. And then the stab of betrayal. The reporter covering the story referenced anonymous sources who had provided him with personal details about me, including a tidbit of information that only one of my new colleagues would have known. Someone had done this on purpose.

Just when I thought things couldn't get any worse, I got to the comments section. My hands were shaking as I scrolled down with dread, not reading through them at first but staring horror-struck at how many there were. Page after page after page. I knew I shouldn't read them, but the self-destructive desire to understand just how badly I had ruined my life was overpowering. I scrolled back up and started from the top. Every comment was more awful than the last.

Her grandmother must be so ashamed of her, read one. It was the worst thing anyone could ever say to me.

There is no way I won't be fired over this, I thought. Why would anyone, let alone the White House, want to be associated with me now? If the photos weren't enough to do me in, the snarky implication throughout the story—that I didn't deserve what I'd accomplished—would. I felt as if every sexist stereotype had been projected onto me at once. I might as well have a scarlet *M* stamped across my chest. I was tainted.

I wasn't ashamed of my time as a model, but the narrative was wrong and the context was missing. I had initially started modeling and acting while I was an undergrad at the University of Southern California. Even though I had received grants, loans, and financial aid, it wasn't enough to cover tuition—let alone housing, gas, and food. So I worked. A lot. Swiping ID cards at the campus gym and hostessing at Miyagi's on Sunset Boulevard until two o'clock in the morning. Yet after being scouted by a talent agent, I discovered a much more efficient way to pay my bills. Acting provided a generous new stream of income; the pay from just one day's work on a Pepsi commercial with Ricky Martin was enough to buy my new computer for school.

After college, I struggled to find a job as a journalist but kept booking acting and modeling gigs. And then *Maxim* called. They wanted to interview me in the magazine as a featured "rising star," and my agent was adamant I couldn't pass it up. I reluctantly agreed to do it, thinking it might lead to a break I desperately needed.

Back in early 2000s Los Angeles, appearing in *Maxim* meant you were an "it girl." But now in late '00s Washington, DC, any overt display of sexiness was a reputation killer. Smart women couldn't—or at least shouldn't—be sexy. Female sexuality and intelligence were made to feel like they were inversely related. "Watch out for the 'skin-terns,'" I had heard around DC, referring to young women who wore fitted skirts or dresses. They weren't considered smart, and they certainly weren't respected. I could only imagine what people would be whispering about *me* now.

My White House badge on the bedside table suddenly caught my eye. There I was, smiling and oblivious, in a photo taken less than a week earlier. It already seemed like an artifact of a past life I'd never experience again. A life I was now disqualified from living. I ran to the bathroom and heaved into the toilet.

Early the next morning, I walked to work in the frigid cold, wearing my boxiest Ann Taylor and expecting the worst. I imagined holding up my badge to the Secret Service agent and it no longer granting me access onto the White House grounds. Maybe someone would meet me at the gate and confiscate it right then and there, like a bad fake ID.

And if, by some chance, my badge still worked, then I'd still need to figure out how to explain this to Mona. I ran through various scenarios in my head. If she called me into her office and asked me about it, I would make sure she knew that the pictures were taken a long time ago. If she fired me on the spot, I would beg her to give me a probationary period instead. Either way, I would apologize to her for the embarrassment of wasting her time during one of the busiest weeks of her life. Tensions were already sky-high to ensure that the president's transition went smoothly.

A thought crept into my mind that the president or first lady might hear about the story, but I pushed it quickly away after a fresh wave of nausea coursed through my body. Puking on the sidewalk outside of the White House was where I drew the line.

In the distance, I saw some of my colleagues walking toward the gate to the West Wing. Were they staring at me? I pictured other staffers—who I had previously thought would be my future friends—gossiping and laughing about the article. Most of them would now see me in my underwear before even shaking my hand.

I had tried to convince myself that everything would blow over quickly in a news cycle that had far more important stories to report on, but Google Alerts were repeatedly pinging my phone. The *Daily Mail*: MEET THE NEW GIRL AT THE WHITE HOUSE (GOOD JOB CLINTON'S NOT STILL PRESIDENT)! Perez Hilton: IT'S GETTING HOT IN THE WHITE HOUSE! Fox News even covered it. The hits—and the stories—kept coming.

Standing on Pennsylvania Avenue at the black metal White House gate, I wondered if maybe this was the side where I belonged. Maybe the commenters were right. I had dreamed too big. It was 11:59, and Cinderella was about to turn back into a pumpkin.

I held up my blue badge to the Secret Service agent inside the checkpoint booth and waited. What felt like several excruciating minutes passed, and then I heard it—*click*—the unmistakable sound of a latch unlocking.

Passing the white-gloved Marine Sentry guarding the West Wing lobby doors, I made a beeline past the Oval to my desk, eyes glued to the floor the whole time.

As planned, I was already there when my boss walked in.

"Good morning," she said, continuing to her office without stopping.

I waited for her to say something, anything, to me over our shared wall, but instead the only sound I heard was papers rustling. An hour passed. Then another. It occurred to me that maybe she was waiting for me to initiate the conversation.

"Do you have a minute?" I asked, sliding into the chair in front of her nervously.

She had a Top Secret national security briefing book open on her desk. Was I really about to bring up something as ridiculous as *Maxim*? But I had to. I was now trending worldwide on Google.

"Sure, what is it?" she said, closing the book.

"I'm sure you saw the story, and I want to explain," I said.

She looked at me with a blank expression on her face, and I realized that she had no idea what I was talking about. That was the one scenario I hadn't prepared for. I told her everything as fast as I could, while my face burned with humiliation. So much for the great first impression I'd planned to make.

"I'm really sorry about this. I don't want to be a

distraction for the White House at such a critical time," I said, bracing myself for her response.

Her expression remained unchanged. She paused for a moment before leaning forward in her chair. What she said next would determine the trajectory of my life.

"As far as I'm concerned, you'll be judged by the quality of your work. Period. Do the work, and you will be fine." And then she reached for her briefing book.

I took the cue.

"Thank you so much," I told her, rising to leave. I was too stunned and relieved to say much more. I was safe. For now.

On one hand, it felt like I'd just been rescued from the brink. There was nothing I wouldn't do now to make her job easier. Yet on the other hand, I was as anxious as ever.

Do the work. It sounded straightforward enough, but would the work ever really be enough?

In the weeks that followed, the knot in my stomach remained. I had never felt so isolated. I was walking the halls alone, eating alone, riding the Metro alone. It was hard for any of my friends to relate to being the recipient of a national media onslaught, so I mostly kept my misery to myself.

"I was told to keep my distance from you," one of my male colleagues said as we stood in line one day to pick up lunch from the White House Mess. Over his shoulder, the door to the Situation Room swung open. There I was, feet away from one of the most powerful spaces in the world, and I felt so small.

I had been trying to convince myself that every cold shoulder and judgmental look was just in my head, but here was the confirmation. Someone had pulled him aside to say it would reflect badly on him to be seen with me. And the rejection wasn't coming from only within the White House.

I thought that despite the lack of acceptance in my new world, I could at least rely on a sense of belonging from those in my old world. But a couple of weeks later, while eating Stouffer's lasagna out of the carton in my apartment, I realized that, like many First and Onlys, I felt like an outsider in both my past and my present.

Since I'd started working at the White House, I hadn't had a chance to connect with many of my close friends or family. I had decided to write a group email letting everyone know about my new job and that I was thinking of them. *Maybe a few words of encouragement will make me feel better*, I thought. Minutes after hitting SEND, I received a reply from my best friend of fifteen years. It was one word and in all caps: UNSUBSCRIBE.

My stomach hit the floor when I read it. What did that mean? Unsubscribe from me? My life? Our friendship?

Alma and I had been close since we met as preteens in the early '90s. We had seen each other through our baggy-pants phase when we were both in "crews," through our college days at USC (me) and LMU (her). In some ways we were opposites—we went to rival schools, we had few friends in common, and she was petite while I'd grown to a lanky five foot seven by age twelve—yet in the ways that mattered most, we were kindred spirits.

We were both Latinas who had immigrant moms, similar upbringings, and a drive to break out of whatever predetermined paths our fraught childhoods may have pointed toward. She had been my touchstone—someone who had seen every identity permutation I had twisted myself into. And I liked to believe that I was hers, by her side through difficult moments in high school, and cheering her on at every step since.

I immediately reread my original email. Had I come off like I was bragging? I didn't see anything that could elicit that kind of response. Over the previous weeks, I had interviewed for jobs, started work, and dealt with the media storm around my old modeling photos. My note was more of a mea culpa for going MIA while in crisis mode. So what was going on? The only thing that made sense was that our lives had finally diverged one step too far. I had suspected as much through the years, but I didn't want to believe it. Or face it.

Our friendship had first started to show strain when I moved away to attend Harvard. I invited Alma to come visit several times, hoping to introduce her to my classmates and sightsee around Boston together.

"I don't want to meet your snobby friends," she finally blurted out on the phone.

Alma never visited during the two years I was in Cambridge, and I rarely went back to LA. I avoided mentioning anything about school or my classmates when we spoke after that. Since there was an entire part of my life that was seemingly off-limits, our calls gradually became more awkward and less frequent. I was at a loss, wondering what I'd done wrong to cause the ever-growing rift between us. She never told me.

I was pretty sure she convinced herself that I had changed. It's a maddening dig First and Onlys often hear from our friends or family back home: "You've changed." I was still the same person inside, but aren't we *all* meant to change throughout our lives? Evolve and become more experienced? The more she pulled away, the more betrayed I felt.

It didn't help that I hadn't received the kind of enthusiasm you'd expect from my family either. As is sometimes the case for First and Onlys, my family didn't seem to have a lot of curiosity about my accomplishments. They were glad I was doing well, but beyond a general "How's it going?" there didn't seem to be a lot of interest in learning more about the experiences I was having. Not at USC. Not at Harvard. Not even at the White House. I told myself that they were just unsure of what to ask and felt out of their depth—and I believe that to be true to this day—but I still felt bummed to be asked about my health, who I was dating, or if I was getting enough sleep, but never about the aspects of my life I had worked so hard to realize.

At the time, I didn't fully grasp that for First and Onlys, our efforts to recalibrate and survive in new spaces can often be misunderstood as leaving our friends, our culture, or our families behind. We face dual rejection—in our new environments and in our old ones—for *opposite* reasons. I missed my best friend and wanted to tell her how out of place and inferior I was feeling. But ironically, she wasn't talking to me because she probably thought I felt superior. I wanted my family to be excited to hear about my life in DC, but other than my mom and my sister, no one else seemed to have much interest.

As my first freezing winter in DC dragged on, I hid at home every weekend and ate more frozen lasagna than I'd like to admit. I lay awake most nights with anxiety-induced insomnia. I reread nasty comments online. I had suicidal thoughts. No matter how many pep talks I gave myself, I still felt like I didn't belong in my own life. They say you shouldn't let other people decide who you are. But with each passing day, it was becoming a little harder not to.

Still, I kept doing my job, Mona's words—*You'll be judged by the quality of your work*—in my head. Showing up to work early, getting things done, being polite and friendly, staying away from drama, leaving work late, and generally keeping my head down. Rinse and repeat for months. My boss seemed happy, and that was all I really cared about.

I told myself that I could get by on my own and tried to detach myself from wanting to be embraced or accepted. But every time I heard of a birthday party I wasn't invited to or a happy hour I was left out of, I felt like a pariah all over again. And then, a moment of kindness.

There was a young woman who sat in the office next to mine who would sometimes stop by while looking for her boss or to ask a question. Kristin was from Montana, with wavy blond hair that she tucked neatly behind her ears, and when she smiled at me, I could tell it was genuine. I looked forward to her random drop-ins every day. Even though we hardly knew each other, she was the closest thing I had to a work friend.

One morning in late March, when the cold was finally beginning to show signs of lifting and the cherry blossoms were about to bloom, Kristin walked up to my desk unexpectedly.

"Hey, wanna go grab our lunch together?" she said.

I thought she was messing with me at first, but then I realized she was being sincere.

I steadied my voice before I answered. "Yeah, I'd love to," I said, trying to play it cool.

It took all that I had not to jump out of my chair and throw my arms around her in a grateful hug.

We walked side by side to the White House Mess, passing colleagues ranging from senior staff to special assistants. I self-consciously studied Kristin and tried to detect any embarrassment she might have about being seen with me, but she smiled and greeted everyone like usual.

When we arrived at the pickup window—where staffers hurriedly grabbed their lunches before heading back to eat at their desks—there wasn't a hint of uneasiness on her face.

"So what did you order?" she asked as we stood in line.

"A tuna sandwich," I said, watching as one of our peers from the chief of staff's office who had picked up her salad from the window walked toward us.

"Hey, Kristin." Pause. "Hi, Alejandra," she said, smiling at us as she passed. It was the first time she had ever acknowledged me in public.

When Kristin and I got back to our adjacent offices, paper plates in hand, she called out to me from the doorway.

"Let me know when you head down to the Mess tomorrow."

"For sure," I said, feeling the urge to hug her again.

Kristin's friendship was a life raft that first winter at the White House. Her solidarity helped disarm the balled-up fist that had lodged itself protectively in my gut. Someone else in my position might have been able to shake off all the silent treatment. But a wound inside me had been triggered, and it was old and familiar. Yearning for belonging.

I had been chasing it for decades; the *Maxim* fiasco was only the most recent—and extreme—example of my failure. It went all the way back to my childhood and the feeling that I didn't even belong in my own family. I was different; I wanted different things. It took me many years to realize that when you are a First and Only, you are set up to advance alone. You often don't belong, by definition.

Many of my peers were fortunate to move through new experiences in a familiar pack, with others who could relate and sympathize. I didn't have a network of individuals who could understand both where I came from and where I'd arrived. Or help me make sense of why every time I "leveled up" after an achievement—meaning I reached a new threshold in my social or economic mobility—there also seemed to be a related emotional cost.

Sometimes it sucker punched me like *Maxim* did, but most of the time it was more subtle. Disengagement from family. Anxiety. Friendships lost. Sadness. Debt incurred. Numbness. A romantic relationship challenged. Insomnia.

For most of my life, I had rarely stopped to take account of what I had gone through or how it was affecting me. I felt pressure to keep up the pace. It's said that when you're skating on thin ice, your speed is your safety. And I took that to heart; many of us First and Onlys do.

But now, here I was at the height of success—the actual White House—and my emotional pain was also at its absolute pinnacle. What was going on? I had been the first in my family to have a number of life-altering experiences. I was supposed to feel free and liberated. So why did it still hurt so much?

I didn't understand back then that the pain was a sign that there were parts of me that remained unhealed. I could work hard and climb high, but no amount of success could reverse the emotional toll that social and economic mobility had taken. In order to move through it—to find my peace and heal—I'd first need to acknowledge it. Admit to how I'd tussled with it. This book is my attempt to dig up those bones at long last. Lay them all across the table. For myself and for any other First and Only who finds themselves blazing trails yet burning inside.

Motivated by the idea that history doesn't repeat itself but it often rhymes, I decided to take stock of not only where but also *who* I came from. Because achieving societal measures of success wouldn't be enough to keep me from repeating our ancestral patterns. I could feel my family's influence looming over me—even as my experiences moved farther and farther away from theirs—and I wasn't satisfied with summing up their lives using the broad brush of "immigrants seeking a better life." There was more there, and I wanted to know what it was. So I started with a question: What were the generational cycles I was born to break?

I found an answer within my family's rhyme.

CHAPTER TWO

BORN ON THE BAYOU

I WAS A COLLEGE freshman the first time I heard the term *legacy*. I knew the traditional definition of the word—something received from the past—but the way my classmates used it to size each other up was more loaded. So-and-so was a "legacy" because they came from a long line of USC alumni and their family's history with the school probably helped them get in. Before then, I didn't think much about inherited advantage. In fact, I didn't really think about inheritance much at all. I certainly didn't know that white households inherit wealth over five times as much as Black households and over six times as much as Latino households. Seeing it so plainly opened my eyes to how our lives are regularly nudged and altered by the experiences of our ancestors. I started to wonder: If everyone has a family legacy, what was mine?

Tracing back the history of your family name can often provide insight into who you are and where you come from, but my last name only left me with more questions.

In 2018, I had just landed in LA after a weekend with friends in San Francisco when I saw I had a message on

LinkedIn from an attractive young Latina. I expected it to be a request for career advice or collaboration, but then something caught my eye. Her last name was almost identical to mine but spelled a bit differently.

I read the message as I made my way through the airport terminal, and suddenly my high from the weekend was replaced with sinking anticipation of new drama related to my father. He—or a distant relative of his—had a way of randomly popping up once or twice a year, and I was feeling increasingly fed up with having no choice but to receive them.

"I know your dad…," she wrote. *That makes one of us*, I thought.

I was a toddler when I first met my father, and he'd been an unknowable man ever since. You never knew when he was coming, you never knew *why* he was coming, and you never knew how long he would stay. He was slippery.

According to my mom, that had been part of his charm in the beginning. When she met him on a dance floor in Marina del Rey, California, he wore dog tags on a long silver chain that—thanks to his shirt being halfway unbuttoned—jingled on his bare chest as he danced. He was mysterious and cocky in the way handsome egoists can be.

I had seen him only about six times in my life, each more confusing than the last. Where did he go, and what did he do for a living? He'd never give me a straight answer. Our most reliable bond was the random call—later, the random GIF—I'd receive around the holidays, always from a different phone number.

"Hello. It's your father," he'd always say, unsure that I would recognize his voice. He had the cautiousness of a man who was used to being hung up on.

But I would never hang up, even though I often wished afterward that I had. I would stay on the phone and listen to him rant about the latest way he was being screwed over by his baby mamas, the government, or his landlord.

"She's trying to sue me for child support!" he'd moan about his various exes, not grasping how weird it was to be complaining to *me* about having to pay child support. "Maybe if you talk to Baby Mama XYZ on my behalf, she'll calm down," he'd slip in.

It made zero sense why he'd want to involve me in his drama, but I felt responsible for shouldering my father's stress anyway, thinking that I would be a "good daughter" if I carried some of his load for him. He would typically call from South America or New York City—always in some sort of trouble and always fishing for help or words of support. It wasn't until I was in my thirties that it dawned on me: He never seemed to ask about *my* life. Our relationship was entirely one-sided. The few times I worked up the courage to call him out, he'd quickly change the subject. Usually to nonchalantly mention that I had yet another new brother or sister.

Why this man kept having so many kids when he wasn't around for the ones he had was beyond me. At my last count, I have around ten half siblings from at least six women. One of my half sisters was conceived when I was two months old. As I write this, a new half sister just reached out to me on Instagram. So when I received a

LinkedIn message from this woman in 2018, I figured she must be yet another long-lost sibling.

"How do you know my father?" I asked over a WhatsApp call with her, cautious to not share my phone number with a complete stranger.

"Well, your dad's dad—your, um, grandfather—married my mom, and they had me…so I guess your dad is my half brother. And that must mean I'm your aunt!" she said, her tone amused. I had previously been told that my paternal grandfather passed away before I was born.

"I wanted to talk to you because your dad showed up at our house asking for money. He told us about you and all the things you've done. And about how he raised you, and the great relationship the two of you have. I looked you up and…I guess I wanted to know if all of that is true."

I felt indignation swelling up in my chest. It was bad enough that my father parachuted in and out of my life, but now he was misrepresenting our relationship as a character reference to get cash?

"No, actually that's *not* true. He didn't raise me and we don't have a good relationship," I told her. I knew I shouldn't have taken the call.

She apologized awkwardly, and we were about to hang up when I couldn't help myself.

"So did you guys give him the money?"

"Noooo. Oh, no. Your dad and his father don't have a very good relationship. It hasn't been the same since, you know"—she paused and then lowered her voice—"the name thing."

I had no idea what she was talking about.

"You know, when your dad started going by the last name Campoverdi? He was in some sort of trouble, but your grandfather was really upset when he did it."

She was so casual in her delivery, she obviously didn't realize that she had just revealed to me that my last name was fake. More than ever, it struck me how little I actually knew about my father. Not even something as simple as his real name.

I suppose I shouldn't have been so surprised. Through the years, he had changed his first and last names several times. Last I heard, he was going by the name Verdi. But I had always thought that Campoverdi was the real one. Turns out, it had no history, no lineage. It was meaningless.

"Huh. Okay, then," was all I could think of to say.

As soon as I hung up with my newly discovered aunt, I immediately called my mom.

"Well, you know your dad lied to me about his name when we were dating, right?" she said, her Mexican accent adorning each word.

"I think so. Tell me again," I asked, shaking my head.

"He said his name was Willy," she chuckled. "He didn't tell me what his real name was until *after* you were born!"

"Did you consider that as maybe…a red *flag*, Mom?"

The women in my family didn't seem to notice some of the biggest, brightest red flags when it came to men. Or maybe they did notice but didn't want to acknowledge them. This was the first of several patterns that emerged as I began unspooling my family's past in an effort to understand my present. As much as I wanted to consider myself independent, I'd come to realize that I'd entered this world within a context. A constellation of legacies already in motion.

Think about it this way. To be alive today, we each come from 2,048 ninth-great-grandparents, 1,024 eighth-great-grandparents, 512 seventh-great-grandparents, 256 sixth-great-grandparents, 128 fifth-great-grandparents, 64 fourth-great-grandparents, 32 third-great-grandparents, 16 second-great-grandparents, 8 great-grandparents, 4 grandparents, and 2 parents. There are thousands of people in each of our family lineages, and their emotional experiences leave a mark on us.

I suppose it was ultimately fitting that I have never been a Campoverdi. In more ways than one, I belong to my maternal great-grandmother, my grandmother, and my mom. I am a continuation of their legacies. I am a Medellin.

***

Before I was born, the lives of the Medellin women set the stage for the family legacies that were passed down to me. These Invisible Inheritances are a part of our birthright. Yet while some people are legacies at fancy colleges or country clubs, First and Onlys often emerge from cycles of instability and adversity. This doesn't discount or diminish the many positive legacies we receive from our families. But by nature, being a First and Only usually suggests that there was an effort to break *away* from something. And that pattern is often written right into how our body reads our DNA sequence.

It turns out that the matrilineal line resembles a Russian nesting doll; the egg that once created us was originally formed inside our mother's fetus while she was still inside our grandmother's womb. Three generations commingled in the same body, blood, and spirit for a moment in time. Epigenetics—the study of how behaviors and environment can cause changes to how our genes are expressed—has explored how trauma can be passed down from one generation to the next, whether from economic insecurity, discrimination, emotional neglect, or any number of hardships. Research suggests that our ancestors' struggles sometimes altered them down to the cellular level, and that those changes were then passed on to us, affecting our own mental and physical health. Even the emotions our moms experienced when they were pregnant with us. This idea really hit home for me when I learned about genograms in grad school.

It was 2007, and I was in the second semester of my first year at Harvard's Kennedy School of Government. Sitting in the back of a classroom with stadium seating, I listened as the professor introduced our guest lecturer of the day, a trained psychologist who worked in leadership. I don't know if I ever paid more attention in a class than I did over the course of the next hour.

Using a whiteboard, the woman mapped out Hillary Clinton's genogram to illustrate how generations of women in her family had experienced betrayal trauma because of infidelity. I couldn't believe how explicit the connections were when you examined the dynamics of family relationships through time. It was like interpreting a visual language from one's ancestors. As the lecturer described her process, I scribbled notes so I could re-create one for generations of my own family.

A genogram is a diagram of your family tree, but instead of showing only birth order and family structure, it maps out the relationship dynamics between your family members. Divorce, hostility, indifference, betrayal, distrust, abuse, control. An illustration of your family's *emotional* inheritances, through generations.

After class, I tucked myself away in a quiet corner of the Kennedy School library, pulled out a blank sheet of paper, and wrote each of my family members' names chronologically in what looked like an org chart. When I came across an experience or a dynamic that seemed to repeat over generations, I used a black Sharpie pen to draw a line connecting every person involved. And then there it was, clear as day: My great-grandmother. My grandmother. My mom. Me. Our family's genogram revealed several bold lines that directly connected the four of us.

Three generations of women in my family had primarily been single mothers. Three generations of women in my family struggled to make ends meet. And then the boldest line, a central thread woven into all the others: Three generations of women in my family had been in emotionally tumultuous relationships with chaotic men.

There it was, one of my family's Invisible Inheritances, unmistakably plain on paper. Falling in love with the wrong man had sidetracked each of their lives in a consequential way. It flowed like an underground river in my family—an undercurrent pulling us for almost a *hundred* years. All the way back to my great-grandmother Maria Elena, who was born in 1907 in the Mexican state of Sonora.

According to my great-uncle, *beautiful* was the word most commonly used to describe Maria Elena, but from the few tattered black-and-white snapshots I've seen, the word I'd use is *intense.* She didn't seem to smile much in photos as a young woman, her dark eyes often downcast or looking off into the distance. Most women of the time would draw fake moles on their faces, using a dot of black eyeliner, but the mole under Maria Elena's lower lip was real. I should know. I inherited her trademark mole in the exact same place.

Maria Elena was raised Catholic and had a predictable middle-class upbringing until she caught the eye of a charming Mexican banker ten years her senior. She was only around sixteen years old when Alfonso started pursuing her with over-the-top declarations of eternal devotion. His love bombing did the trick. Maria Elena fell hard for his worldliness and fedoras, and in the early 1920s, they married and moved to Nogales, Arizona, where he found work as a bank manager.

Not long after, the drinking started.

Alfonso had a habit of coming home drunk, yelling angrily, and throwing things around the house. Unfortunately, my great-grandmother was already pregnant with her first child when she realized this. Alfonso never laid a hand on her, but the verbal and emotional abuse kept Maria Elena in a constant state of fear throughout her pregnancy. How trapped she must have felt to be two hundred miles away from her family, in another country, when her dream man turned out to be a nightmare. How humiliating and hopeless it must have seemed.

One night, Alfonso came home more intoxicated than she'd ever seen him and yelling so violently she feared he'd hurt her and the baby. Even though she was in her last trimester, she left their home that very night and traveled the next day to stay with her parents, who happened to be temporarily stationed in Los Angeles while working in a diplomatic capacity for the Mexican government. Alfonso followed her to LA, begging her to return, but she refused. He was the love of her life, but that didn't matter anymore; she had a baby to protect. They soon fell out of touch and Alfonso remarried not long after.

Choosing to become a single mother at nineteen years old in the 1920s was gutsy. She would need to find a job and face the stigma of being a young divorcée, but she was willing to do that and more if it meant keeping her daughter safe. That daughter, my grandmother Maria Louisa, was born not long afterward, in 1927. She became our family's first US citizen by birth.

———

Maria Louisa—Abi, to me—was born in LA but raised in Tijuana, Mexico. She was barely out of diapers when Maria Elena's parents' work for the Mexican government ended and the whole family trekked back across the dusty border. Yet in the 1930s, the boundary between the US and Mexico was porous. Abi grew up with one foot in each country, attending school on both sides of the border and even working in a US factory during World War II. Every morning, Abi boarded a yellow school bus that was idling by the San Ysidro border and traveled to San Diego to attend classes at Sweetwater High. She spoke fluent English with no trace of an accent, thanks to her binational education.

Abi adored two things—her mother and art of any kind. When she wasn't at school, she'd be directing the neighborhood kids in her original stage plays, sewing their costumes, making paper dolls, writing poetry, sketching, devouring books, and watching American films at the local theater. She was obsessed with Mickey Rooney, Judy Garland, and Shirley Temple. Yet she often found herself wondering about her father—where he was, what his new life was like, and if she ever crossed his mind.

When Abi was twelve, Maria Elena found work in a factory in Tijuana and caught the eye of its well-to-do owner. They married not long after, moving Abi out of her grandparents' home and into an upgraded lifestyle. She was already a sought-after date with the boys in town—thanks to her pin-curled hair, heart-shaped face, and sweet-natured personality—but now that she could afford stylish new dresses and white gloves, her popularity soared.

By the time she was barely twenty, Abi was engaged to her best friend's brother Paco, who also happened to be her next-door neighbor. On paper, he was everything she wanted—dependable and safe, with jet-black hair and a fashionable mustache. Her life was mapped out flawlessly. She'd live close to her parents and raise a family alongside her best friend's children. But unbeknownst to Abi, she had inherited a powerful predisposition, and it was about to make itself known.

Bernardo was wearing a white button-down open to his belly the day Abi first met him on the streets of

Mexicali, Mexico, while on vacation with her family. He was just six years older than she was, but unlike anyone she had ever known. Born and raised in Germany by his Mexican businessman father and his German mother, Bernardo spoke four languages and went to school in Chicago. By the time his family moved from Germany to Mexico, he was a trained civil engineer. Yet his sophisticated upbringing and intellect didn't dim the hustler energy about him. He had a street urchin's spirit in a Clark Gable body.

The summer day they met, Bernardo spotted Abi on the street and trailed her for blocks in his car, mesmerized by the bounce of her hair, the sway of her skirt, and the confident way she held her shoulders. When she ducked into her destination—the local movie theater for one of her beloved matinees—he parked his car, bought a ticket, and sat down in the row directly behind her. By the time the movie ended, they somehow had plans to go get ice cream together. One week later—after a whirlwind of chaperoned dates on horseback and on a boat that had MARIA spelled out in roses on its canopy—Abi and her family returned home from vacation to find Bernardo in their driveway on one knee. He had beaten them home, determined to make Abi his wife. She called off her engagement to Paco and accepted Bernardo's proposal on the spot.

Not long after, Abi learned that Bernardo had a habit of drinking and disappearing.

Every time it happened, she knew where to go. She'd search the local dive bars one by one until she found him, and then she'd bring him home. It must've been painful for my great-grandmother to watch Abi head down the same agonizing path she did. But if she ever pulled my grand-mother aside to warn her, Abi didn't listen. In her wedding portrait, my grandmother is wearing a high-necked white satin gown and her eyes are sparkling with joy. Through the years, when anyone questioned Abi's relationship with my grandfather, I'd always hear her say the same thing: She loved him "no matter what" and would stay with him "until the end." And she did.

Even when he gambled away the horse and cattle ranch he'd inherited and they had to move into a con-crete shed with no electricity or hot water, behind his sis-ter's house in Mexico City. Even when Abi gave birth to my mom and five other children and he'd disappear for months at a time, leaving her to raise their kids alone with no clue when he'd return or send money. Even when the lack of help, resources, and time put a stop to her sketch-ing, writing, and reading. Even then.

If it was romance that drove my great-grandmother and grandmother into the arms of troubled men, it was my mom's dream of coming to the United States that set her own birthright legacy in motion.

For my mom, Cecilia, to dance was to live. As a child, she wasn't the top student in her class, she often went to bed hungry, and her patent-leather shoes had holes in their soles, but when she danced, she forgot everything and radi-ated like a star. My mom once told me that her most painful childhood memory was the time she was given the lead role in her elementary school dance performance but couldn't afford the costume. The part was given to someone else, who had the money. After that, she became convinced that the only way to fulfill her dream of becoming a professional dancer—or any dream for that matter—was to go to *el otro lado*. The other side of the border.

Since my grandmother had been born in Los Angeles, my mom technically had dual Mexican/US citizenship, and the sheer proximity of an alternative reality tortured her. Sometimes she'd visit my great-grandparents in San Diego during the summer—where they had a house thanks to a lucky gamble at Tijuana's Frontón Palacio. She wanted nothing more than to live in that magical land of manicured lawns, swimming pools, and Pizza Huts.

As a teenager in the 1970s, my mom could physically see the US from their house in Tecate. Abi would come home from teaching English to Tecate Brewery workers and watch my mom take off on her bike, through the brush and up a hill to the border, carrying her cheap transistor radio. Once at the border, she'd raise the radio over her head in the air until it picked up the signal from American stations. She would stand like that for hours, listening to Janis Joplin, the Rolling Stones, and the Beatles until her bony arms shook.

Creedence Clearwater Revival's "Born on the Bayou" was one of her favorite songs to sing along to—never mind that she didn't understand a word of the lyrics coming out of her own mouth. She was so set on her American Dream that she even had special clothes put aside for the day she'd finally make the move up north. Tucked safely in the back corner of her only dresser drawer was a dainty sweater with red cherries embroidered on it. Unworn and folded with care.

When my grandfather started taking odd jobs watching the boats of wealthy businessmen in Marina del Rey, my mom saw it as her chance to make her move. She would do anything to go to California, she told my grandparents. Work anywhere. When she was eighteen years old, they agreed to let her go under one condition. She'd work in a car mat factory that was managed by her uncle, so he could keep an eye on her.

Cecilia had attracted a lot of attention in Tecate—always wearing the same black leather jacket and decorating her jeans with rhinestones and strips of black velvet—and she was also naive and far too trusting, a bad combo that worried my grandmother. My grandfather reassured Abi that my mom would be working long hours in a well-supervised job, and then drove Cecilia across the border in his dilapidated Chevy Impala as it poured down rain. The Impala's windshield wipers had long been broken and were permanently stuck in the left position, so my grandfather tied a rope to the tip of one of the wipers and had my mom repeatedly pull it to the right through the passenger-side window—the whole way from Tecate to Compton. When he finally dropped her off at her uncle's apartment, her arm might've felt like mush but she was happy—and wearing the sweater with the cherries on it, her long nails painted a matching ruby red.

The hairnet, rubber gloves, and ogling men on the line at the factory may not have lived up to Cecilia's vision of Hollywood, but her perspective changed the moment she received her first paycheck. She blew the whole thing on trendy corduroy bell-bottoms from Montgomery Ward. Word of my mom's new wardrobe got back to Mexico, and it didn't take long for her three sisters, suitcases in hand, to show up on the doorstep of the trailer home she'd moved into.

An ad in the *Los Angeles Times* for factory work assembling cash registers lured the four sisters west to Santa Monica, but at the time, they had no idea they were moving near the beach. When my mom walked out onto the breezy pier and saw the blue-gray Pacific Ocean for the first time, she felt like she had finally "arrived." The sisters found an apartment together where the air smelled like the sea, they papered their bedroom walls with tacked-up magazine clippings of male models, and they bought white roller skates with neon wheels. They had the perfect bachelorette pad— until Abi missed her daughters too much and announced that she and my grandfather were following them over the border and moving into their apartment. Lured by Abi's cooking and the prospect of much cheaper rent, everyone settled together in a small apartment on Marine Street, at a busy intersection where Santa Monica bordered Venice.

The Medellin sisters couldn't speak English yet, but they didn't let a small detail like that cramp their style. They hustled all angles, wringing every last drop out of the opportunities that were available to them. It was a Latina *Sex and the City*: Aunt Nannette with her high cheekbones, Aunt Sofia with her hourglass figure, and Aunt Elizabeth with her long, dark silky hair. They competed in and won beauty pageants, with Nannette crowned

Miss Baja California in 1979 (free travel and hotel stays!). They worked retail on what's now the Third Street Promenade (discounts on the best clothes!). And they appeared in the local newspaper for no apparent reason (the caption under the photo simply referred to them as "Mexican Beauties"). They were even extras in the 1970s Chicano gang movie *Walk Proud*, posing in halter tops as *vatos* in lowriders cruised by in the film's opening sequence.

It was all going according to plan for Cecilia, who had come to the US ready for her close-up. Seizing every opportunity to be onstage, she joined several dance companies and entertained tourists as one of the regular skate dancers at the famous Venice Beach Roller Skate Dance Plaza—always in Daisy Dukes and wearing her signature shade of magenta lipstick.

On the weekends, the four sisters would fight over space in the one bathroom mirror before going out dancing in rayon-blend minidresses and heavy eyeshadow. It was on one of those nights that "Willy," a uniformed Navy man wearing a smug expression under his trimmed mustache, approached Cecilia on the dance floor. The name of the nightclub? Destiny.

Cecilia danced all night with Willy, attracted to his exoticism (as an Ecuadorean who was raised in Queens) and impressed that he could keep up with her disco-plus-salsa moves. In the months that followed, he showered her with expensive dinners, furs, jewelry, and clothes. While the presents he gave her never seemed to have price tags on them, my mom convinced herself that they weren't stolen. The upscale three-piece suits he wore on their dates were obviously expensive and tailored, so she figured he must have been the successful New Yorker he said he was. Still, he never introduced her to any of his friends and consistently dodged personal questions whenever she asked about his background.

After dating on and off for over a year, Cecilia couldn't shake the feeling that something wasn't right about Willy. It was around the same time that she also realized that she was pregnant with me. When he heard the news, Willy offered to marry her and take her back to New York to live with him, but her gut said that going would be a mistake. She told my grandparents that she would rather be a single mom than live alone across the country with a man she didn't really trust. But my grandfather was old-fashioned. As an unwed mother, it was her duty to marry Willy and move to New York, he said.

The thought of leaving LA and her family while she was pregnant terrified my mom. Her nerves killed her appetite, and she began to lose weight at the very time she should've been gaining it, which only made her worry about the health of her baby on top of everything else. She developed perinatal depression and insomnia, often crawling into bed next to my grandfather in the middle of the night and begging him through tears to let her stay.

He refused, so she turned to the Virgin Mary instead. She asked *la Virgen* to grant her a miracle—a child who was born healthy *and* the blessing of her father to stay in LA. *"Virgencita, protégenos,"* she'd say.

She prayed so hard and so often that it wasn't unusual for her to wake up with a rosary still wrapped around her hand. She even started wearing a small gold medallion of *la Virgen* on a chain around her neck at all times, as an offering to God.

Finally, when she was in her last trimester with a huge pregnant belly, my grandfather gave in. She immediately started eating again, gained weight, and was able to sleep. In fact, weeks later, she went into labor while devouring a tall stack of pancakes with Abi at Norms diner. They rushed across town to Cedars-Sinai hospital together (because Cedars took California's Medicaid insurance), and Abi stayed by her side every second of her thirty-hour labor.

When I was finally born—healthy—my mom declared that *la Virgen* had indeed granted her miracle. "A miracle child," she proclaimed, swaddling me in her arms. "Destined for something special." When she brought me home from the hospital, it was to the three-bedroom apartment where both of my grandparents and all four Medellin sisters lived.

Every inch of that apartment was occupied, from the living room stacked with bikes to the balcony banister where our laundry was drying. My mom jokes that I was never put down as a baby, only passed from one outstretched set of arms to another. Much like our family's Invisible Inheritances.

———

Sitting in the Kennedy School library with four generations of my family mapped out on a table before me, I saw young women with big dreams at the beginning of their lives. And then I saw their options clawed back by their relationships with unpredictable men. They chose young, fast, and impulsively. And, undeniably, they chose similarly. I realized a hard truth: I had done the same. Professionally, I had been the first generation in my family to cross several thresholds. But there's a difference between changing your outer life circumstances and coming to terms with your inner emotional life.

As I made my way home through Harvard Square at dusk, I had to admit to myself that many of my own past choices about men had been the same as my great-grandmother's, grandmother's, and mother's. Here I was, a supposedly empowered woman, yet at times I had continued the family legacy of tolerating mistreatment from charismatic men. What had been modeled for me in the past—imprinted upon me—had led me, unconsciously, to repeat the same patterns. "I got it from my mama," the flip side. As much as I wanted my family's Invisible Inheritances to end with me, it also felt overwhelming to be the one responsible for breaking all the generational curses.

Thankfully, I noticed another recurring familial theme that followed closely behind each messy relationship. When they were on the ropes, the women in my family summoned unwavering tenacity. One walked away from her abusive husband while she was pregnant, one raised six children with little to no support, and one chose to raise her child alone rather than alongside a man who lied to her. I had inherited a legacy of generational strength and wisdom as well. Walking up to the two-story townhome I shared with four of my classmates, I knew that the lines that connected me to the women in my family had also led me to Boston. To uproot myself and move far away from home in search of something better. To end relationships that were rooted in control rather than love. Choosing myself, no matter who or what I lost, or how painful it was at the time. Like they had.

Ultimately, gaining knowledge over my Invisible Inheritances—the bad and the good—opened up space for more mental and emotional freedom. We may each have ancestral legacies, yet understanding what they are, and deciding which ones we'd like to continue or disrupt, allows us to then challenge their power more intentionally. It gives us agency. That's the thing about epigenetic changes: not all of them are permanent. Our choices, behavior, and environment can still make a difference. And that has been a big part of my journey as a First and Only.

We all have ancestors whose steps lead into ours, but our lives haven't already been written. We heal generational trauma when we choose to evolve versus repeat, creating new inheritances for generations to come. Changing the future for our own bloodlines.

Each day, we have the choice to become a better ancestor.

CHAPTER THREE

AMOR ETERNO

THE MORNING AFTER my grandfather smashed all the dishes from the kitchen sink onto the linoleum floor in a fury, Abi called for an emergency novena.

Abi, my mom, my three aunts, and I knelt in a circle between my aunts' twin beds and begged God to stop my grandfather's drinking. At five years old, I didn't really get what all the commotion was about. I thought my grandfather, whom I called Abito (short for *abuelito*), was fun. He was always slipping butterscotch candies into my hand when no one was looking, and calling me his *muñequita*. When I started taking piano lessons, he saved his meager salary for months to buy me a piano to practice on. He could even eat the pickled jalapeños and carrots Abi left in a bowl in the middle of the kitchen table with his fingers without flinching. (No one else dared to even try them.) And whenever he'd find a daddy longlegs in our apartment—which was more often than I would've liked—he'd capture it in the palm of his hand and place it on top of his bedroom pillow. *"Mira, que no tengo miedo,"* he'd say as I squealed, hands over my eyes.

Yet watching all the women in my family whisper Hail Marys under their breath with furrowed brows and palms turned up to heaven, I could feel tension seep from their bodies into mine.

"Dios te salve, María. Llena eres de gracia."

The lumpy brown shag carpet dug deep into my knees, leaving red indentations, as I knelt by their side, but I didn't dare complain. Instead, I just quietly shifted my weight back and forth, from one side to the other, and chewed on my cuticles until they were raw. My grandfather was still sleeping in the next room.

Our novenas, a Catholic tradition that consists of nine days of focused prayer for a specific intention, were always directed to *la Virgen*. Abi told us that a novena to the Virgin Mary was the most powerful and gave you the best chance of having your prayers answered because she was the Mother of God. And who didn't listen to their mother?

That scene—gathering together and feverishly praying—is one of the most familiar of my childhood. We always asked for the same two things: for money (*"Que cambie nuestra situación económica"*) and for my grandfather to stop drinking.

It helped that our apartment had the trappings of a makeshift church, complete with *veladoras* in the sink, a depiction of the Last Supper by the kitchen table, and two large paintings looming over us on the wall: A classic image of Jesus on black velvet, his serene gaze raised toward the heavens. And an iridescent guardian angel in a white robe hovering protectively over two frightened children as they cross a crumbling bridge. Both common images in the homes and wallet cards of Mexican immigrants.

I spent a lot of time staring up at those paintings as a child, particularly during the novenas we prayed in their shadow. The sense of calm I felt emanating from them was in complete contrast to the regular pandemonium that otherwise characterized our cramped apartment.

Whenever Abi, my mom, and my aunts gathered on their knees with bejeweled rosaries in their hands, I'd join the edge of their circle and wait for an angel to appear or some other miracle to happen. For twenty minutes, they'd recite prayers in a chorus as their bodies swayed like stalks of wheat in the wind. When their fingers reached the last beads of their rosaries, I'd scan the room to see if anything had changed, but we remained the same, as we'd always been—a motley crew of overwhelmed strivers.

In those days, you couldn't walk from one side of our home to the other without dodging a person, a stuffed animal, or my aunt Elizabeth belly dancing in the living room. Different lengths of women's hair were shed everywhere— the carpet, the sink, and the shower. My playroom was not really a room at all—it was a narrow coat closet with my toys wedged inside. And there was rarely a silent moment. Since our three-bedroom apartment housed six adults and one child (me), there was an undercurrent of melodrama and activity at all times—in Spanish.

How are we making rent this month, who has a hot date, does anyone understand these forms, don't play with Abito when he drinks, meet my new boyfriend, so-and-so needs to find a job, how do we get health insurance, let's go to the beach, Jesús and *la Virgen* will protect us, everyone load the rolling laundry cart so we can walk to the laundromat. Our home was a rowdy mash-up of styles, personalities, and stages of life, all set to the soundtrack of Abi's beloved Juan Gabriel. Abi would often blast Juan-Ga's megahit "Amor Eterno" while she cleaned the house, tearing up because it reminded her of her mother—just as today, my mom and I play the same song and think of her.

The upside to living with so many adults as the only child? The love. Every birthday was a big deal, usually consisting of a piñata party at Marine Park, with my mom leading the games, Abito manning the piñata rope, and Abi serving the carne asada, rice, and beans. All the presents under the Christmas tree were for me. My cheeks were often painted with the kisses of my many aunts, and even though I winced whenever Aunt Elizabeth came at me with her lips covered in pink gloss or when they'd take turns parading me around the house on a leopard-print pillow, I secretly loved the attention.

It seemed like the only person I was related to who *didn't* live under our roof was my father, but as grandmothers in single-parent households often do, Abi immediately stepped in to fill his place. Just as her own grandmother had done.

As co-parents, Abi and my mom could not have been more different. Abi was in her early fifties when I was born, with cropped chestnut hair and a nurturing disposition that was usually doled out in the form of thick, steamy tortillas and lemon meringue pies.

"Made with love," she'd always say when she served us,

white flour still on her hands from shaping the masa. And her love really did make the food better, the way orange juice tastes sweeter out of a wineglass.

Abi was the only person who would get on her hands and knees to play with me on the floor. I loved how the green veins on the tops of her hands would pop out under her paper-thin skin when we played My Little Pony. She always smelled like Pond's cold cream, sweet and baby-powdery. Her dedication to being my grandmother was so deep she stopped dyeing her hair and was completely gray by the time I was two, so she could better look the part.

My mom, Cecilia, on the other hand, was twenty-five when she had me and often referred to herself as a "bohemian." When I picture her in those days, it's usually mid-laugh with white roller skates permanently attached to her feet, '80s hair sprayed to a crisp, magenta lipstick, and some variation of bright-colored spandex. Always up for fun, obsessed with the Venice Beach Boardwalk, and very much in need of a mom herself. I remember how odd it felt to walk down the street as a little girl next to my mom as catcalls, whistles, and car horns trailed us.

In many ways, Abi's moonlighting as my surrogate parent gave my mom permission to keep chasing her version of the American Dream. When it was time to buy her first car—ideally something dependable to shuttle me to and from school—my mom bought her fantasy zippy sports car for $500 instead. Why was it so cheap? It had no engine. She eventually saved enough money to have one installed but couldn't afford to repair another "minor" issue. Every time we turned left, the front passenger door would spontaneously swing wide open, like the yawns around the house the morning after the Medellin sisters went out dancing. But my mom had a way of painting everything as an adventure.

"Get readyyy," she'd tell me as we neared a left turn.

When the passenger door lurched ajar, I'd cling to my seat with all my strength—hard pavement whizzing by—and we'd shout in unison: "Open sesame!"

Everything my mom lacked in judgment, she made up for in resourcefulness. On Halloween, she insisted we go to "where the good candy is." In Santa Monica, that meant north of Montana Avenue, one of the more expensive neighborhoods on the Westside of LA. She'd drive around until she found the best block and then encourage me to slip into the crowd of local trick-or-treaters streaming into yards with lifelike graveyards, fog machines, and bowls filled with full-sized Kit Kats and Milky Ways.

"Go! If you don't ask, you don't get," she'd say, nudging me, long chandelier earrings glittering in the moonlight.

When my aunt Nannette landed a gig as a Spanish-language entertainment reporter for a Latin American network, my mom became an expert at snagging every complimentary "media ticket" she could get her hands on. She took me to Disneyland two to three times a year, Disney On Ice, Universal Studios, the LA Zoo, and the Los Angeles County Museum of Art. We saw productions of *Cats*, *Phantom of the Opera*, and *Annie*. All completely for free. She may not have been able to afford buying me the Lunchables I begged for, but I went to more theatrical performances and amusement parks than any kid I knew.

My mom even found ways to finagle me into weekly dance and piano classes at a huge discount. And when my dance studio offered students the chance to appear as paid extras in movies, she quickly signed me up, leading to my blink-and-you-miss-it cameos in the 1988 films *Mac and Me* and *Purple People Eater*. My favorite part of being an eight-year-old child actor? The free soda and snack table.

Every weekend, we were hiking in either Temescal Canyon or Will Rogers State Park, and we never passed a garage sale my mom didn't stop at to search for gems. Yet all her initiative still couldn't mask the polarity between how carefree our lives appeared on the outside and the reality at home.

My grandfather Abito's new life in the US highlighted his failed expectations of himself, and measuring his fluctuating levels of unhappiness was our home's emotional weathervane. In Mexico, he had always been known as a sharp and gifted fixer, sought out by men of influence, but his thick German/Mexican accent, dark skin, and nebulous work history were too much for employers to look past in 1970s LA. After a life spent gunning for his big break, he couldn't find work. At least not work that he thought was worthy of him.

When he looked in the mirror, he no longer saw the dapper stranger who swept Abi off her feet during a matinee movie in Mexicali all those years ago. These days, he was typically in a khaki zip-up jumpsuit covered in grease, from his part-time job as a car mechanic in a run-down body shop, and holding a Heineken. When he hugged me, I'd hold my breath as the inside of my nostrils burned from the strong scent of gasoline in his hair and clothes. The skin on his face, chest, and arms had turned a permanent brownish red from grueling days in the sun and too many nights at the bar, and his black hair had grown coarse and gray. Yet despite the salt-and-pepper stubble that dotted his chin and cheeks, his face was still masculine and striking—like a faded movie star you can't quite place. He was impatient and gruff, and I adored him completely. I never understood why everyone seemed to be scared of him when the sun went down.

Mornings in our apartment were generally even-keeled; Abi cooked breakfast while whistling "Jeepers Creepers" or some other jazz standard from her childhood, and people left for work, with perhaps an argument or two between sisters about who had worn whose clothing without asking. The witching hour didn't usually arrive until around 7 p.m. It was then that Abito would stumble through the door, reeking of cheap beer, and proceed to—in my mom's words—"throw a fit."

The body shop he worked at closed at four, and it was just across the street from our apartment, so the later he came home, the worse shape he'd be in. Abi would pace the living room as the hours passed and leave a plate of beans and tortillas out, but it didn't make much difference. Filled with liquor and regret, Abito would look for reasons to be angry when he got home—the house was a mess, there wasn't enough food, or there were dirty dishes in the sink.

Sometimes I'd stand there watching everyone fight, too stunned to cry. And sometimes my mom and Abi would tuck me away in my bedroom before Abito came home. Either way, I was the only person my grandfather never yelled at.

The nights I was preemptively hidden in my bedroom were the worst. One of the first things Abito would do after bursting through the front door was try to find me so we could play. Since I wasn't in the living room, he'd stumble over to my bedroom, only to find that the door had been locked from the inside. I stood there bewildered behind my mom and Abi as he'd bang and kick the door with all his might while yelling desperately. *"¡Mi muñequita, abreme la puerta!"*

There was pain and confusion in his voice as he'd call out to me, and I wanted to open the door, but Abi and my mom had their bodies pressed up against it. The door hinges would creak, and I'd watch them jerk back with each of my grandfather's forceful shoves. *"¡Dios mío!"* Abi would exclaim as the door inched open despite their best efforts. It was two against one, but Abito was still stronger.

Then, in an instant, the apartment would become bizarrely still. I could sense Abi and my mom's lingering fear as they slowly backed away from the door, but I didn't share it. I just wanted to be with my grandpa.

Needing a sanctuary in the middle of the constant commotion, I'd find ways to create my own. I would play for hours on the living room floor with my plastic Fisher-Price figurines and lose myself in detailed plots and episodic stories that would go on for months, like the Univision telenovelas we watched at night. I dreaded the days when Abi vacuumed, because she'd put my toys away and destroy weeks of world building. I'd cry facedown in bed, inconsolable at the hideout I'd lost. Abi and my mom were mystified by my utter devastation. They didn't understand that the elaborate fictional world I'd built was my escape, similar to my fantasy of being Cinderella while sweeping sidewalk leaves.

My other refuge was the row of tattered Shirley Temple VHS tapes that sat on our bookshelf, the most well-worn being *The Little Princess*. At least one night a week, Abi would turn off all the lights in the living room and we'd snuggle up in the dark, losing ourselves in the story of a bighearted little girl who was orphaned and thrust into poverty when her father was killed in the war. Abi and I were kindred spirits—a pair of hopeless romantics with absent fathers—and we loved the surprise-twist ending. Spoiler alert: Shirley's father wasn't dead after all, and he returned home, scooping Shirley up in his arms and rescuing her from a life of destitution. It was a happily ever after that Abi and I wanted to believe in.

The books that she gifted me, all of which were her own personal favorites, were similar in theme—cross-class fairy tales or romances. *Jane Eyre* was the one I liked best. I could tell that it made Abi happy when I read the large hardcover book with green page edges. She'd sneak a peek at me from the kitchen and smile when she thought I wasn't looking.

When I lost myself in my make-believe worlds, I knew what to expect each day, and I could recognize what was happening. In real life, my child brain had no ability to process the constant ups and downs, particularly when it came to money.

Each month, our access to cash—and therefore food—fluctuated at a nerve-racking cadence. The first half of the month we were generally all right. Everyone would get paid and contribute $200 to rent and $20 to food. Abi would go to the market and buy the staples for the household—meat, milk, rice and beans, and soup—and sometimes a Gansito snack cake or a jar of cajeta for me. Those items would last us for a couple of weeks, and then we would usually run out of money again. Our rent was reliably late while Abi stretched the food we had as far as humanly possible, finding ways to incorporate beans as the centerpiece to every meal. Eggs with refried beans. Bean soup with queso fresco crumbled on top. Rice and beans. Bean-and-cheese burritos.

Yet despite her efforts, the fridge mostly sat empty during the second half of the month—with the exception of a tiny section of food that was labeled with my name, thanks to the food stamps my mom had set aside. I felt guilty whenever I opened the fridge and saw my little section, and I started tracking how much food there was (or wasn't) in the house. I remember visiting a childhood friend who had a pantry—and standing inside of it, marveling at the ceiling-high shelves filled with uneaten food. It was like being in the supermarket. There were people who had so much food they could just leave Kraft Mac & Cheese and Pop-Tarts sitting there unopened? I couldn't fathom being that rich. We bought our food on an as-needed basis, and you knew to hurry up and eat it before someone else did.

The instability in my environment started to feel like a problem I had to solve. I saw hemorrhaging around me—from money to food to energy to options—so I made myself the tourniquet. Many First and Onlys, especially the children of immigrants, may relate to developing an exaggerated sense of responsibility and self-sufficiency during our childhood as a survival mechanism. We essentially become a Parentified Child—enlisted into the role of family care-taker. This was certainly true for me. My default mode became "save and rescue."

I became the family helper, translator, doctor ques-tioner, form filler, concept explainer, living dictionary, and therapist. Whenever I saw someone washing the dishes, I'd insist on pulling over a chair to stand on (so I could reach the sink) and help. I developed a heightened sensitivity and learned to scan people's moods constantly—noticing sub-tleties in their body language and showing up however the moment asked for.

But parentification can also be emotional. For me, this looked like providing emotional support to my caretakers—giving out advice, mediating between them, and hiding my own feelings in order to not stress anyone out. I thought being a "good kid" meant expressing no needs of my own and "managing up." And I was *great* at it. I became an expert at dimming myself in order to preserve emotional oxygen for everyone else. When you're a child in a dysfunctional home, it's in your own best interest to keep the peace by managing the adults around you. Even if it's at the expense of yourself.

It didn't help that it felt deceptively rewarding to be a "little adult." I felt valued and valuable when I took care of my elders. "You're the reason I live, Alejandrita," Abi would tell me. My mom said the same. It was a lot of pressure, but it also made me feel like I was a vital part of my fami-ly's survival—a thought that was further validated by the amount of time and money they poured into my education.

Abi and my mom always tried to give me what they thought was the best and, in their minds, that meant going to a private Catholic elementary school. Yet even after finding their dream school and successfully applying for need-based financial aid, Abi still had to take a job as a teacher's aide to help pay down the last of my tuition. It was the single largest investment either of them had ever made.

Saint Monica Catholic Elementary School is north of Wilshire Boulevard in Santa Monica, near the neighborhood we'd drive to for the good candy on Halloween. The Spanish-style schoolhouse is next door to Saint Monica's Church, a massive limestone cathedral that was built in the 1920s and has a parish center designed by Frank Gehry. Needless to say, cost was already an issue before classes started. Watching my mom rummage through used clothing bins for a plaid school uniform skirt close to my size was the first indication that I was different from the other kids. The second happened in the classroom.

Since Spanish was my first language, and the only one we spoke at home, I struggled to keep up in kindergarten. When my test scores began to lag behind those of the rest of my classmates, the teacher figured I had a learning disability and put me in the lower reading group. Abi would not have it. She made a rule then and there that everyone in our home, including my grandfather, could speak only English to me. Abito struggled to pronounce words in English—"Gyoot morrrrrneeng," he'd say to me at breakfast—but Abi was firm. And it worked. She had me in the advanced reading group by Christmas.

Each morning, Abi and I would board the Big Blue

Bus #3 in front of our apartment building, and she'd lead me in reciting a prayer to the Sacred Heart of Jesus as we rode down Lincoln Boulevard to school. Right before we said goodbye, she'd make the sign of the cross on my forehead so God would protect me, like she did every time we were apart for more than a few hours. Sometimes, Abito would leave work early so he could drive me home in his tattered Chevy Impala, with its ripped seats and peeling exterior paint. On those days—I'm ashamed to admit—I'd duck down and pretend to tie my shoes when we drove past my classmates. Abito would glance over at me, and I'd tell myself that he had no idea what I was doing. But I know now that he must've. It had taken only one year in school for me to learn I had a reason to feel embarrassed.

My self-consciousness, my hypervigilance, and the pressure I felt to look after my family all piled up and soon began to take a toll. First and Onlys are sometimes exposed at a very young age to a number of environmental factors that can lead to a dysregulated nervous system— from neglect and loneliness to poverty and severe stress. And I was no exception. I was five years old when I had my first panic attack. It was the year my mom got a boyfriend.

Chad was a rookie cop in the LAPD, who looked like Arnold Schwarzenegger in his prime and was ten years younger than my mom, which made him about twenty when they first started dating. I despised him at first sight.

"She's just jealous," my mom and aunts would whisper to each other.

They assumed that since Chad was the first guy my mom had ever brought home consistently, I simply didn't want to share her attention. But that wasn't it. The truth was, I wanted a dad more than anything. The stable and loving kind. Chad wasn't either of those things. He constantly talked about himself yet barely spoke to me, open-mouth kissing my mom in between inflated stories about the police academy. When I was around him, something deep inside my stomach rebelled, like it did at Magic Mountain when I looked up at the biggest, twistiest roller coaster. I now know that it was the first time I ever felt my own intuition.

It wasn't just that Chad was dismissive of me; he wasn't all that nice to my mom either. He would make snide comments about her body and say she needed to lose weight, once telling her that she wasn't as skinny as she thought herself to be. I had a nagging feeling that he'd end up hurting her somehow, and I became all the more protective. Where was she going? Was she upset? Did he do something to her? Even escaping into my toy closet couldn't distract me from my obsessive worry.

On one of those nights, my mom spent an hour primping in front of the bathroom mirror as I sat on the closed toilet, admiring her. She had a date with Chad, but since it was pre–"open sesame" days and neither of them owned a car, they'd often hang out only a few feet outside our front door, at the bottom of our apartment building's exterior stairwell. As she scrunched her mane of spiraling curls with Dippity-do hair gel, her smoky-black-shadowed eyes looking straight out of a magazine, I thought she was the most glamorous woman in the world.

"Don't go," I blurted, feeling an overwhelming urge to grab on to her leg.

"I'll be back soon. We're just going to talk on the stairs," she said, filling our tiny bathroom with a tear-inducing cloud of Aqua Net. "You'll be fine."

I went to my play closet and tried to be "well-behaved," per Abi's instructions, but as an hour passed, a spine-chilling sensation rose through my body, similar to the feeling you get while lurching toward the ground on a giant Ferris wheel. Then my hands started to shake, and it suddenly was hard to breathe. I was completely overwhelmed with an urgent need to do something—anything—to get to my mom.

Running to the front door, I did what I knew I wasn't supposed to do. I went outside to the top of the stairs and looked down. The path to the bottom of the stairs was a pitch-black column of nothingness—no light and no sound. At the end, I could barely make out two shadowy figures, their mouths pressed together and their backs turned to me. I summoned my courage and called out weakly.

"Ma, come here." My heart was pounding double time.

"Go inside and close the door," she said, completely oblivious to the terror in my voice.

I wanted to tell her that I was sure I was dying, but all I could muster was, "Come upstairs, please." Tears were streaming down my cheeks now, as I became more desperate.

"What did I tell you? Go inside!"

I could tell I was annoying her, but this was an emergency. I started to beg. *"Please, please, please come."*

We went back and forth like that for a few minutes—me begging, her telling me to leave them alone. When I went back inside the apartment, I was dizzy, nauseous, and my heart was still beating out of my chest. As a five-year-old, about the worst thing I could ever imagine was that my mom wouldn't be there when I needed her. I cried in the closet until my panic attack subsided, but the shock and powerlessness I experienced left a mark. A living wound that would be reopened years later, when my father sent for me.

My father may never have paid child support, but when I was eleven, he bought plane tickets for my mom and me to visit him in New York City. I had been on the East Coast only once before, when Abi took me to New York so that he and I could officially meet for the first time (I had no memory of seeing him as a toddler). I was eight back then and I remember visiting Queens to meet my dad's mom (another grandma!) and being impressed that she owned a laundromat. She cooked me soup and gave me presents, which helped offset the agitation I felt radiating from my father. It was as if I was keeping him from somewhere he needed to be—at all times. Three years later, I wondered why he was sending for me again if the last time seemed to be so annoying to him.

Sitting on the plane waiting to take off from LAX, I was flipping through the SkyMall catalog when I heard the outside cabin doors close with a whoosh. As the flight attendant made her way down the aisle checking seat belts, all of a sudden I couldn't hear anything. It was as if I were underwater. The loudspeaker, the people in the seats around me—everything was muffled. And then it happened again.

My heart pounding furiously. Fire in my veins. Not enough oxygen. My hands shaking. And this time, a high-pitched ringing in my ears that grew louder and louder with each second that passed. Our plane had shrunk to the size of a coffin, and it felt like I was being buried alive.

"I want to get off!" I pleaded to my mom.

"What are you talking about?" she asked, her mouth agape.

"I need to get off the plane now! Open the doors! Let me off the plane!"

Almost on cue, the plane pushed back from the gate and started slowly rolling toward the runway. There would be no getting off until LaGuardia.

I spent the next five hours in the throes of one big panic attack. Unsure how to help me, my mom rang the flight attendant, who gave me a brown paper bag to breathe into. For once, I didn't care who was looking at me or judging. Halfway through the flight, I became so dizzy that I spent the last hour lying on the cold metal floor in the back of the plane. All I could think about was getting out of the air and on the ground.

When we arrived at my father's apartment in New York City, he listened to my mom's recounting of what had happened and shook his head in exasperation.

"*I* know what happened. It's because you're malnourished! You're too skinny," he said.

I waited while this insistent stranger with a slicked-back ponytail lined up a dozen plastic cups of juice on the kitchen table and told me that I was not allowed to get up until I had finished each and every one.

"It's good for you," he said, softening a bit. "Listen to your father."

Your father, I thought. Hearing the word come out of his mouth felt good. My stomach was still in knots from the plane, but I wanted him to like me—love me, even. Plus, it was the first time I'd ever seen both of my parents in the same room and only the second time I'd ever spent time with my father. I wasn't going to ruin it by complaining. I would show him what a dutiful daughter I could be. One by one, I did what I was told and choked down each cup of juice, eyes watering and stomach churning, as he counted.

Twelve drinks in a row. When I finished the last juice, my father looked pleased, and I felt nauseated, but I kept it to myself. By that point, I was getting pretty used to swallowing things down for the people I loved.

"You're going to have your own room. It'll be great," my mom said while packing up our things to move to the apartment that she and Chad had rented in Venice. After five years of dating, they were engaged, and I was about to be a preteen bridesmaid. Their ceremony was set to take place at my elementary school's church and gym. Everything about the wedding—and Chad—was majorly invading my space.

I didn't want my own room. I wanted Abi at the kitchen table, flattening mounds of tortilla *masa* with a wooden rolling pin. I wanted our Shirley Temple movie nights, Abito's secret candy stash, and Marine Park down the block. Our apartment was the only home I'd ever known, and even with its turbulence, it was way better than feeling like the third wheel in my mom and Chad's newlywed love nest. Just a few miles away, our new two-bedroom apartment might as well have been on another planet, as far as my comfort level went. Plus, I could feel that Chad didn't want me there.

"Do we *have* to go?" I implored.

"Yes. You'll see. Everything is going to work out."

I wanted to believe my mom. She was supposed to be the one who knew best. But one week before the wedding, she was moving boxes into our new apartment when she walked in on Chad. Having sex with a waitress. In *my* brand-new bedroom.

Gift-wrapped presents had already started arriving by mail, and a wedding dress was hanging in our closet, but my mom didn't hesitate to call the whole thing off—with just days to go. It was over, and I was free. I think I smiled for a week straight, out of relief. In true Medellin fashion, my mom's picker might've been off, but her backbone wasn't.

A few mornings later, I heard sniffles coming from the lower mattress of the trundle bed we shared, and I climbed down to cuddle with her. She tried to hold in her tears, which made her shoulders and the bed shake like there was an earthquake. It scared me to see her like that.

"We'll be okay. God and *la Virgencita* will help us," she said, rubbing her wet nose with the back of her hand. It was what she and Abi said whenever anything bad happened.

Something in me changed after that. Witnessing my mom's devastation while at the same time realizing that my gut had been right all along made me double down on being our family protector and mediator. Turns out, I *had* known better. Maybe there was more I could've said or done. Maybe I could've prevented all this from happening. I told myself that I would be wise enough for the two of us from here on out. By the time my grandparents' wedding anniversary came around the following year, I had fully bought into my role.

I knew that we were going somewhere special because my mom dressed me in my Sunday best—a long white dress with a lace ruffle at the hem, paired with a brand-new pink headband. Even Abito wore a button-down shirt. We arrived at the nicest restaurant I had ever been to, dim with high-backed red leather booths and matching crimson cloth napkins. Someone ordered a bottle of champagne, and I was mesmerized by the glittering coupe glasses on the table. My aunts, Mom, and Abito happily chatted away across our crescent-moon-shaped booth, yet my eyes were fixated on Abi.

She was upset about something. No one else was paying attention, but I could tell. I followed her eyes as she looked back and forth from Abito to the table. I read her body language, her shoulders hunched toward him almost in anticipation. He didn't notice or so much as look her way. She had three strands of black-and-white fake pearls around her neck, a big departure from her usual casual button-down shirts and slacks. It was obvious she had made an effort to look nice, wearing earrings and even a new blue dress.

Overtaken by an idea, I leapt out of my seat and reached for my grandfather's right arm. He gave me a strange look as I lifted it up and away from his side and then draped it around Abi's shoulders. All the emotions she had been holding back suddenly came bursting out of her eyes as grateful tears while Abito kissed the side of her head.

At the time, I felt proud of what I'd done. Abi and Abito were smiling, and I felt the tension at the table vanish like the bubbles in our champagne. Now, I look back and see a kid surrounded by adults yet consumed with worry about *their* well-being. Trying to fix *their* pain. Losing touch with her own experience because she was too busy putting herself in everyone else's shoes.

It would be their last wedding anniversary. Not long after, my grandfather was walking home from the body shop in the blazing-hot sun when he had a major stroke. He collapsed on the sidewalk, and, shockingly, no one stopped to help. People likely assumed he was homeless, because of his oil-stained clothes and his disheveled appearance, and just walked around his body and went about their business. By the time someone finally checked on him, it was too late.

I watched numbly from the other side of the hospital glass as, days later, Abito was disconnected from life support. He had been the only man of our house, albeit a tormented one, and I was his *consentida*, his favorite. He was the closest person I had to a father, and then one day, he was gone. It only added to my certainty that I could be abandoned at any moment.

Abito's death knocked our home off its axis. Abi had always been everyone's rock, but now she was overcome by grief, crying at odd times throughout the day. She started wearing Abito's wedding ring next to hers and refused to take the bowl of pickled jalapeños and carrots off the table, even though no one else liked them. Our evenings were much quieter with Abito gone, yet they also felt oddly emptier. No one was stumbling through the door at night, pulling us all out of our rooms and into each other's business. Apparently, our chaos had also been our glue. And there was one less paycheck pitching in on rent and food, making it that much harder to fill the fridge each month.

Over the next few years, our household gradually broke up and emptied out. My mom watched longingly as her sisters got married and moved away, and I knew it was just a matter of time until she found someone new herself. She had been the first to get engaged, and now she was in her midthirties, with an unused wedding dress burning a hole in her closet. But as badly as she wanted out, I wanted to stay near Abi. Each time my mom had a date, I'd brace myself. There was the slick lawyer and also the country-western dancer, but none of them ever stuck. Until Mario, that is.

Mario walked into her life at exactly the right moment—or, in retrospect, the worst. At the time, my mom was working as a secretary at a local bank, where Mario was an accountant. She quickly caught the attention of the men in the office, and Mario didn't waste time, inviting her to be his date at a fancy dinner for the bank's executives. Awkward and overeager, he impressed my mom with his degree from UC Berkeley, despite the fact that he didn't have the swagger of the men she typically dated. I wasn't sure what to think. He wasn't as obviously problematic as Chad, but they seemed to argue a whole lot for two people in the honeymoon phase. Both were strong-willed single parents with unresolved baggage from their past relationships. So of course, in a little over a year, they were engaged.

Soon after the wedding, my mom and Mario bought a small but charming white house in Santa Monica with a shingled gable roof that looked like something out of "Hansel and Gretel." She finally had the house and the husband—it seemed like my mom's happy ending.

I actually allowed myself to get excited too. I'd been an only child, and now I had an older stepbrother and a younger stepsister overnight. *And* a future sibling—since my mom became pregnant months after their honeymoon. My ten-year-old stepsister, Cindy, was a goofy daddy's girl, with long black hair to her waist and a closet full of pastel T-shirts. And my thirteen-year-old stepbrother, Mario Jr., was the big brother I always wanted—a troublemaker, who went to public school, owned a paint gun, and had cassette tapes of all the latest West Coast hip-hop. But our storybook house with antique furniture and dainty white lace curtains soon became a war zone.

A few months in, it was clear that the marriage was already unraveling. My mom and Mario fought on a regular basis about everything and nothing, their clashes escalating in intensity as the weeks passed. I started to recognize my grandfather's bloodshot drunken eyes in Mario's face. My mom would sometimes come to my room after their fights and shut the door, unloading to me about how frustrated she was with her husband and complaining about how combative my stepsiblings were becoming.

At twelve years old, I wasn't sure what she wanted me to do with this information. Was I supposed to help? Intervene? Comfort her? I could see the battle lines being drawn—it would be our family of two versus their family of three.

Everything caused an intrafamily fight: Who left a mess on the table. Who was on the phone too long. Why I had the biggest bedroom. Who was playing music too loud. Whose dishes were in the sink. My mom instituted a rule that everyone was responsible for washing their own dishes, and soon after, her magenta lipstick tube went missing. Cindy had swiped it so she could set my mom up by putting lip prints on the rims of all the dirty glasses in the sink.

We lived like five adversaries forced to coexist in some sort of cruel reality show. When personal things from my room started to go missing, my mom bought a big brass padlock with a chain and installed it on my bedroom door. She meant for it to make me feel safe, but instead it made me feel like I was under siege.

It was bad enough that every other girl in seventh grade seemed to be buying a training bra except me, and that Bobby—the cutest boy at school, whom I'd had a crush on since kindergarten—had publicly dumped me over lunch break after just one date. But now, Abi lived across town and I didn't have our leaf sweeping, movie nights, or daily bus rides to turn to for sanctuary. As if to say *"enough,"* my body literally recoiled in protest and my spine twisted itself into an S shape, seemingly overnight. As Dr. Gabor Maté says, "If you don't know how to say no, your body will say it for you through physical illnesses."

Every doctor we saw agreed that surgery was the only

option to correct the severe case of scoliosis I'd developed out of nowhere. The eight-hour procedure would involve placing stainless-steel rods permanently along the length of my spine and fusing several vertebrae. Not exactly how I wanted to spend the summer before eighth grade.

I woke up from the operation tripping on morphine, with a long scar from the nape of my neck to my tailbone and one on my hip from a bone graft. Even though the surgery was a success, my doctor advised I spend the next few months mostly confined to bed, as I regained my strength and learned to walk again.

My body felt as though it had just turned a hundred years old overnight, bolts of lighting landing on my nerves and joints every time I moved, but I decided I'd keep the pain to myself and never complain. I was incapable of shielding my mom from my stepfather's attacks, so I figured the least I could do was not be a burden at home. I'd get up to shuffle stiffly to the bathroom in flannel pajamas and then head straight back to my room, listening for tense voices as I passed the living room and feeling useless.

One night, about six months after the surgery, my mom came into my room to let me know that we would all be sitting down for dinner as a family. We never ate dinner together and I trudged from my bedroom to the kitchen tentatively, wondering what the catch was. There was a platter of grilled fish from Costco in the middle of the table and I eyed it suspiciously, since I grew up around the idea that ordering takeout was a luxury. But there was no special occasion; it was a "just because" meal, meant to give us all a chance to bond.

For a moment, we were just the typical family around a dinner table. A mother, a father, and their kids. I had always wanted to experience that sense of normalcy. *This feels nice*, I thought.

"Does anyone want ribs?" Mario asked, bringing over a container of leftovers from the fridge.

There were only two left—one rib was thick and juicy, with lots of meat, and one was mostly bone.

"I'll take one," my stepbrother said.

Looking over at me, my mom nudged, "Do you want one too?"

I hesitated. Any wrong move felt like it could set off our powder keg of a household.

"Uh…okay," I replied, immediately regretting it as I watched Mario stick his fork into the big rib on the platter and place it on Mario Jr.'s plate. He set the bare bone on mine.

"Why did you give *my* daughter the one with no meat?" my mom snapped at Mario. I looked at her as if to say *Please leave me out of this* with my eyes.

My stepfather's face turned the color of red clay. He pushed back from the table violently and left the room. From where we were sitting, we could hear the front door open and then slam shut. I felt sick to my stomach that I'd somehow ended up in the middle of their fight. I didn't even want another rib.

Ten minutes later, we were still sitting in silence when Mario reappeared, carrying a full tray of ribs from the corner store.

As he unwrapped the package, he glared over at my mom and then at me, with fire in his eyes.

"Does your spoiled-bitch daughter want some ribs?" he shouted. "Well, here you fucking go!" He gripped the sticky ribs with his bare hands and hurled them across the table—directly at me.

The hot meat struck my face and chest forcefully before landing on the floor.

I froze, terrified. My mom, stepbrother, and stepsister stared at me in shock as I wiped barbecue sauce from my face and hair. I couldn't cry, I couldn't speak. All I could think was, *What did I do that was so wrong?* Then I took off running to my bedroom as fast as my still-healing body would allow, locking the padlock behind me. I could hear raised voices coming after me down the hall.

"Open up!" my mom called out as she banged on the door.

Her face was tearstained when I let her in, Mario right at her heels. They went at each other again, shouting nose to nose, like two boxers gearing up for a fight. I'll never forget the sight of them in each other's faces.

Without warning, Mario raised his right arm high in the air to strike my very pregnant mom. They had argued viciously before, but this was the first time he had ever attempted to hit her. Before he could land a blow, as he clearly intended to do, my stepbrother grabbed both of his arms and held them behind his back. Mario, now unable to move his arms, began to spit repeatedly into my mom's face, his saliva landing in streams on her cheeks.

"No, no, no!" she cried, covering her face with her hands.

I felt rage surge through me. "Fuck you!" I shouted, lunging between them. I hadn't moved my torso like that in months, but the adrenaline masked most of the pain.

"Let's go, Dad. Come on! Let's go!" my stepbrother pleaded, pulling his father out of my bedroom. Mario looked pale, and his eyes were glassy.

Padlocking the door behind us, my mom pulled me over to the bed, her arms wrapped tightly around me. I felt the cold grip of numbness all of a sudden. Like a dark hole had appeared inside my chest.

"We're leaving," she said, her voice shaking. "This is it. I'm getting us out of here."

And she did. My pregnant mom left Mario, just as her pregnant grandmother had left her own abusive husband. By the time my baby sister, Monica, was born a few months later, my mom and I had already moved into an affordable housing unit on the same street I grew up on, a few blocks away from Abi.

We never really talked about what happened that night, and I was more than happy to keep everything buried. It scared me to hear my mom and newborn sister take turns sobbing in the middle of the night while I was trying to sleep. Abi would come over regularly to help, but the concern on her face as she washed our dishes and cooked her sopa de albóndigas only made me feel worse. As did the prescription pill bottles that appeared in my mom's bathroom, and the fact that we always kept our window shades down.

Mario pretty much checked out right after their separation, and it was just the three of us now—along with Abi's doting drop-bys and tamale deliveries. My mom had planned to support us with her secretarial job, but soon after leaving Mario, she was laid off. Desperate for help, she started seeing a therapist, who immediately certified her as clinically unable to work. The three of us would end up living off her mental health disability benefits for the next two years.

I remember opening up the front door on Christmas morning to find a cardboard box filled with food and wrapped toys sitting on our doorstep. When the card revealed that it was from the Santa Monica Fire Department, I felt dueling emotions—happiness for the much-needed help and embarrassment that we had become charity cases.

"Monica is the only good thing that came out of that marriage," my mom would say, unpaid bills in hand, and I had to agree. Since the day she came home from the hospital, Monica's natural default expression was a wide toothless smile, and despite what we'd recently been through, we couldn't help but smile back at her. I adored my baby sister instantly, calling her Potato because of her perfectly round and brown face. I lugged her around town on my hip so attentively, people on the street mistook me for a teen mom.

In a lot of ways, I did feel like the mom. At just thirteen years old, I felt like I'd become the de facto head of our household, out of necessity. I needed to protect my mom, and now I needed to protect my baby sister too. Yet a new thought started invading my mind, one that I'd mostly pushed away up to that point. I needed to find a way to start protecting myself.

Back then, I had no real understanding of what it meant to be a Parentified Child, and I knew even less about its lingering emotional aftereffects. Now I see the signs all over. In the hypervigilance I developed as a child, which later morphed into people-pleasing. In the emotions I hid as a child because I didn't want to rock the boat, which later morphed into sometimes denying my own needs. And in the sense of duty I felt to perform grown-up tasks as a child, which later morphed into having a lack of healthy boundaries.

These types of overcompensation behaviors can often be tied to having gone through adverse childhood experiences (ACEs), traumatic events that come in many forms, from neglect and substance abuse to violence and food insecurity. According to a groundbreaking study in the 1990s, led by doctors Vincent Felitti and Robert Anda, experiencing ACEs can lead to excessive activation of the nervous system, a myriad of chronic diseases, and other future health issues. Not to mention the impact of the social determinants of health that are often related to ACEs, such as community violence, discrimination, and housing insecurity. Going to therapy would've provided a safe environment to process and cope with the ACEs I was exposed to, but as is the case for many First and Onlys, my family generally brushed off the mental health consequences of our experiences at the time, a dynamic that can often be cultural.

It would take many years to understand why I felt emotionally responsible for my family members. This is likely because parentification trauma—something that many First and Onlys experience—is often downplayed as simply the byproduct of being the "responsible one" or "the overachiever" in the family. But the reality is much more complex.

In 2021, the song "Surface Pressure," from Lin-Manuel Miranda's film *Encanto*, exploded in popularity, with many people relating to its portrayal of an older sibling who felt a debilitating responsibility to carry all of the family burdens. Thousands of people—and First and Onlys in particular—reacted on social media saying they felt seen for the first time, some referring to themselves as the "family therapist" and the "third parent," some lamenting having to memorize their parents' passwords for them. It was surprising to see the number of people who had experienced parentification yet still didn't have language for this invisible childhood trauma.

I've seen parentification chalked up to "oldest-daughter duties" or simply the role of the "firstborn," particularly in immigrant families. In some cultures, firstborn children are explicitly expected to be the ones to take care of the family. But the complex experience of being a Parentified Child shouldn't be normalized, or minimized as something that simply goes with the territory of being an older sibling, because in reality, there's more to it than birth order. A middle child, an only child, the youngest, or even a cousin can all find themself as the one roped into carrying out emotional labor for a family.

Acknowledging my own experience as a Parentified Child was never about pointing fingers or assigning blame. Parentification is rarely done with malicious intent, and in my case, I truly believe that everyone was doing the best they could with what they knew and had. Yet parents can work hard to provide for their children *and* those children can still end up shouldering an inordinate amount of responsibility. This realization led to a better understanding of just how unusual and upside-down some of the dynamics of my childhood were.

Why is this important? Because our own emotional experiences *matter*—even, and especially, as a child. If no one said that to us then, well, we can say it to ourselves now. We can have the courage to stop putting ourselves last, despite past conditioning or ongoing family dysfunction. We aren't betraying our families when we take care of ourselves.

In time, I came to understand that erasing my own experience wasn't virtuous; it was self-abandonment. And abandoning yourself is never an act of love. But thirteen-year-old me hadn't learned that yet. All I had then was a burned-out feeling with no name and, as I saw it, only one option: harden myself in order to survive.

CHAPTER FOUR

KEEP THEIR HEADS RINGIN'

1993 WAS A good year to be young and angry in Los Angeles. Dr. Dre's album *The Chronic* had just come out, and we were in the aftermath of the Rodney King trial and the LA Riots. The stage was also being set for an explosion of anti-immigrant backlash due to California's Proposition 187, a ballot initiative designed to deny undocumented immigrants access to public education and healthcare. I was thirteen and a summer away from starting high school at the same school I'd been attending since kindergarten. And I was pissed off. For a lot of reasons.

I thought I had done my part. I'd held it together through my mom's separation from Mario, acted like the stoic rock of our little household, and kept my grades up. So when some of my friends and their moms started applying to LA's most prestigious private high schools, I didn't hesitate to join them—poring over my essays and imagining what it would be like to start over someplace new. I'd been in class with the same thirty or so kids for nine years at that point.

When I visited one all-girls campus in particular, I was convinced I'd seen the perfect high school. It looked like a fancy hotel, with a café that might as well have been a real restaurant and five acres of actual grass. In contrast, my current school had an asphalt playground that doubled as the church parking lot. Not only would going to this new high school increase my chances of getting into a good college, but the girls walking around looked like they had just stepped off the pages of *Seventeen* magazine.

It wasn't until my acceptance letters arrived that reality hit. There was no way we could afford any of these schools. In the '90s, the tuition at elite LA high schools was around $10,000—per year. My mom had assumed I'd be given significant financial aid, but the small grants the schools offered wouldn't even cover one semester. I'm sure there were scholarships we could've applied for or pipeline programs to take advantage of, but like many First and Onlys and their parents, we had no idea how to access those resources. So I turned down my acceptance to that perfect high school and tried not to feel left out. I told myself that I didn't want to be at a rich-kid school anyway, which made me feel like I was the one rejecting *them*. *Those kids are spoiled and fake*, I thought. *I'd rather be broke and real.*

But most of all, I was pissed off because I needed to be. When I was angry, I didn't feel as scared.

To distract me from my disappointment—or to keep me from lying around all day watching hip-hop music videos on MTV and The Box—my mom enrolled me in an acting class during the summer of '93. Or at least that's how it was billed to me. In reality, the Virginia Avenue Project was an arts nonprofit with a mission to help "at-risk youth" develop confidence. But I ended up developing an infatuation with cholos instead.

The day my mom and I first pulled up to Virginia Avenue Park in her gold Honda Accord, my center of gravity shifted. Virginia Park is in Santa Monica's Pico Corridor, a working-class community that sits on the edge of the always-congested 10 freeway and is home to the majority of people of color in the city. Back then, it was also one of the central meeting places of a gang on the Westside.

As we got out of the car, I spotted about a dozen Latino gang members in their teens and early twenties huddled around a set of picnic tables at the far end of the park, sitting on the tabletops with their Nike Cortez planted on the benches. I could make out their smooth-shaved heads even from a distance. They were carbon copies of one another, all wearing bright-white T-shirts with baggy jeans or khaki pants, and square-framed black Locs sunglasses. A perfect storm of danger, indifference, and broodiness. The I-don't-give-a-damn energy and air of authenticity they were giving off was everything I wanted to embody. I was captivated.

I noticed a stocky younger guy standing off to the side away from the group, hands in his pockets, looking out across the grass as if he were daydreaming. Something about him felt familiar. He seemed to look over my way, and for a split second I could've sworn we were staring right at each other. I turned away, blushing hard, but couldn't help taking another peek. He was still gazing in my direction. Maybe the summer wouldn't be so bad after all.

Once a week, my mom dropped me off and I'd walk through Virginia Park to class, always squinting to see if I could spot the stocky guy again in the crowd. Since we rehearsed in a rec room encased in glass, I had a perfect fly-on-the-wall perspective. All through class, I'd watch the benches where the cholos hung out, but he never seemed to be there. I started to think that maybe I had imagined the whole thing. Him, the moment we'd shared, the tingling in my chest. But it had felt so real, so I kept on searching.

One day, I looked through the glass doors and then froze. The guys weren't alone this time. They'd been joined by a half dozen girls, who were draped over them like over-sized plaid flannels.

I had studied the extras in Dre's "Nuthin' But a 'G' Thang" video enough times to know that these girls looked exactly the way I wanted to—tough, sexy, and obviously Latina. Unfortunately, I couldn't have been more the opposite. At five foot seven and under a hundred pounds, I'd been called Toothpick in junior high. When I looked in the mirror, I saw an awkward flat-chested dork who could pass for a white girl. I wanted to give off Brown and Proud energy, laced with a little "Don't mess with me," and these girls did it effortlessly. Even from a distance, you could see they had caramel skin and curves, with their skintight bodysuits tucked into baggy pants. And the gangsters were all over them.

Up until that point, my only experience with boys consisted of an eight-year crush on my blond-haired, blue-eyed preppy classmate Bobby. The one who dumped me after one date. I realized that if I wanted to attract the kinds of guys who sat across the park, I'd first need to do something about my face.

My mom still wasn't sleeping through the night, so when 8 p.m. rolled around, she'd call for lights-out and insist that our apartment be as silent as a tomb. I wasn't even supposed to flush the toilet after she went to bed. Paranoid about waking up both an insomniac and a finicky baby, I'd park myself on the couch in the dark and watch music videos on mute, memorizing every frame of Eazy-E, Tupac, Dr. Dre, and Snoop Dogg. Then I would tiptoe into the bathroom and infiltrate my mom's makeup bag to try to mimic the look of the girls in those videos, drawing a black border around my eyes and a brown border around my lips, both with Cover Girl eyeliner. I'd stare at that alternate version of myself in the mirror, someone I didn't recognize in the best possible way. I liked the girl I saw looking back at me.

Makeup became my war paint that summer—black eyeliner, thick mascara, dark-brown lip liner, and light-brown lipstick that were discarded by my mom. When I traced my eyes and lips with black and brown lines, it felt like I was putting on a shield to protect myself. I didn't want to be sensitive anymore—the one who would feel everyone else's feelings for them. That girl had been padlocked inside her own bedroom for her safety. I wanted to know what it felt like to be the one on the other side of the door. Better yet, on the other side of the park.

If makeup was my war paint, baggy pants were my armor. Midway through the summer, my mom took me to

Santa Monica Place to buy a pair of new jeans. I had let her dress me until that point—usually in sweaters and vests, tapered jeans, and girlie dresses. It was one of the ways I had tried to keep the peace when I was a child. While she went through the women's clothing racks, I wandered over to the men's section and came back with size 40 pants. I was a size 0.

"I want these ones," I told her, handing them over while they were still folded. I was hoping she wouldn't unfold them, but she did. They were as wide as a blanket.

"These pants are huge! What do you mean you want these? They don't fit you." She looked at me like I had two heads.

"This is what people are wearing now," I said. "I *need* these pants."

I don't know why she bought them, or the other humongous pairs I got, or the stomach-baring crop tops and big gold hoops from Contempo Casuals, or my black pager from Costco, or why she took me to get French tip acrylic nails at the Fox Swap Meet in Venice. Maybe she felt guilty that all of her attention was on my baby sister, or maybe she simply wanted to make me happy. Either way, my transformation from uniform-wearing nerd to wannabe chola happened over a matter of months that summer.

Hanging out at the park didn't just introduce me to cholo culture and street gangs; I started drinking there too. Which was pretty funny, considering that my acting class was held in the Police Activities League Youth Center, run by the Santa Monica Police Department. With a pool table, a large-screen TV, dirty pleather couches, and armed police officers scattered around, PAL felt more like a halfway house than an after-school program for public school kids. But it was there, only a few feet away from a dozen cops, that I'd sneak beers with a group of fellow middle school kids.

Once or twice, someone brought a six-pack of room-temp Zima—very exciting to those of us who were pretending to like beer—yet we mostly drank whatever castoffs kids could find in their parents' fridges.

Apparently, our little drinking parties didn't go by *completely* unnoticed. The head police officer, seeing me go out back with a cluster of snickering boys, assumed we were up to something else. One day when my mom came to pick me up, he pulled her aside to tell her she needed to put me on birth control immediately (never mind that I was thirteen and hadn't had my first real kiss yet). Thankfully, she shut him down with five words: "I know my own daughter."

I even tried my hand at shoplifting that summer— although turns out, I wasn't very good at that either. On the first try, I was caught stealing a brown Almay lipstick at the supermarket and ended up dramatically handcuffed next to the dairy aisle. Seeing my mom cry as a security guard banned me from shopping at Lucky's for all eternity, I swore to her that I'd never do it again.

And I kept my promise. I had dreams for the future, and although the specifics weren't clear to me yet, I knew I didn't want to jeopardize anything. At the same time, it felt like I'd found a way to connect with my culture that was authentic and real. And cool.

I was a *conflicted* wannabe chola, after all. One whose self-worth was still tied to being the overachieving golden child of her family. I had unconsciously paired cultural pride as a Latina with gang culture—while being told that studying and getting good grades meant you were "acting white."

Who I was and who I wanted to be felt like mismatched puzzle pieces, but I was determined to make them both fit.

———

"Today, each of you are going to write a play," Leigh said, cropped white hair framing her makeup-free face. At five foot ten in Birkenstocks, she was the tallest woman I'd ever seen.

As the founder of the Virginia Avenue Project and our acting class teacher, Leigh oversaw the dozen or so mostly Brown kids and the mostly white professional actors who volunteered to spend time with us each week. The actors had names I'd never heard before, like Kendis and Wolfe, smelled like essential oils, and told us often how much they believed in us. And I could tell they meant it. At the beginning of each class, we'd stand in a wide circle and play theater games like "passing the sound," or we'd crawl around the ground pretending to be wild animals. I hated every second of it at first. And then I was given a pen.

"What do I write about?" I asked Leigh, a stack of blank sheets of paper in front of me. Other than lovesick poetry about Bobby, my writing experience had previously been limited to regurgitating book reports.

"Anything you like. But the best writing is about what you know. Just start there, and see what comes to you," Leigh said, walking away to help the other kids.

I glanced across the room at Alma, who had quickly

become one of my closest friends after we'd met in VAP earlier that summer. She shrugged, her black hair swinging in a ponytail. Everyone around us looked confused, and no one was writing.

What did I know? It didn't feel like I knew much of anything. What did I feel? Numb. I'd been biting my nails for a good twenty minutes when it hit me that maybe that's exactly what I should be writing about: nothingness.

After that, the words started pouring out of me at such a rapid pace, I could hardly scribble fast enough. I wrote a play about a thirty-three-year-old woman named Annette who was fresh out of a breakup and struggling with debil- itating depression. Sound familiar? Only her depression was actually another character named Nothingness, who paid her a visit one particularly lonely night. After working on my play for several weeks, I handed the final product over to Leigh. She read it over with a smile on her face, nodding throughout.

"How did you come up with this? Nothingness being a character," she said, handing my now-formatted-and-typed play script back to me.

I shrugged, not sure how to explain how intimately acquainted I'd become with nothingness in my day-to-day life.

"It's almost…film noir!" she said. I had no idea what that meant, but from her tone, I knew it had to be good. "Great job. No changes."

It was way better than getting an A on a test. In my mind, I'd written a fictional play, yet I still felt like I'd told the truth somehow. Gotten something off my chest. At home, I had to pretend like I wasn't affected by what my mom was going through, but in the safety of my characters, I could give voice to everything I was experiencing. It wasn't quite therapy, but it was the closest I'd gotten to it.

With our plays now done, Leigh assigned each of us a director and professional actors, and we went into dress rehearsals.

VAP had struck a deal with UCLA's Little Theater to hold performances of our plays at the end of the summer—complete with lights, real costumes, actors, and original music. As the playwright, I was given a seat on the stage itself: a folding chair with a small desk, facing directly out toward the crowd. When the theater darkened and blue lights illuminated the stage, I alternated between watching the actors and looking out over the audience, while my private thoughts were scattered around like confetti. It felt as if the audience was reading my diary. What it was like to live with someone as they teetered on the edge and faced their own darkness. As the lead actress performed the last lines of dialogue, it occurred to me that maybe I had exposed too much, been too open. Maybe everyone had figured out that it was about me. Maybe my mom knew it was about her. Maybe I sounded like a crazy person.

Suddenly, the audience rose to their feet in applause. Their reaction felt amazing, even though I didn't really get what exactly they were so enthusiastic about. I joined the actors at the center of the stage and held their hands, taking an awkward bow.

A few minutes later, I was walking through the audience, searching for my mom and baby sister, when I felt a tap on my shoulder. I turned around to see none other than Angela Bassett standing there, lit from within and radiant, with braids spilling down her back. The lead actress in my play had just appeared in the Tina Turner biopic *What's Love Got to Do with It*. She had mentioned she was friends with Angela Bassett, but I never thought anything more of it.

"Hi. I'm Angela," she said with a wide smile, shaking my hand. "I really enjoyed your play."

"Thank you," I replied softly. Everyone was staring at her, but she was looking at me.

"I want you to know how much I personally related to what you wrote. Thank you for your courage and honesty."

I was stunned. It seemed inconceivable that a famous Hollywood star could identify with my thirteen-year-old problems, but there she was saying so. Thanking her again shyly, I walked off, feeling seen.

From that point on, the way I related to my own pain changed. In the theater that night, I'd absorbed the lesson that revealing something vulnerable to others could lead to a sort of mutual alchemy. Not only would I feel less alone in my sadness, but I could create a connection to others, who, in turn, would also feel less alone. If I could transform pain into something positive, then I wouldn't be at the mercy of whatever happened to me anymore. It made the awfulness of what I was going through with my mom feel like it actually had a purpose. I can see now that my love of storytelling came from internalizing that message. And not a moment too soon.

By the time I started high school that fall—at the same

school I'd been attending since kindergarten—I was fully in the throes of my Bicultural Balancing Act. I was searching for a sense of belonging, more than anything, but I wanted it from both teachers *and* troublemakers. And I wasn't willing to compromise one for the other.

Walking onto the schoolyard at lunchtime as a freshman felt like a choose-your-own-adventure novel. Depending on which direction you went, the whole story would end up different. There were cliques already forming—the white skater kids at the tree, the football players on benches by the snack bar—and then I saw them. Off to the far side of the yard were the friends of my dreams. There were about a dozen Latinas sitting on the steps of the library, looking just like the cholas I'd seen at Virginia Park, with their acrylic French tip nails and liquid eyeliner. Even their blue plaid uniform skirts were rolled at the waist several times to skim their thighs. *These are my people*, I thought. Unfortunately, they didn't agree.

I tried to sit with them, but right away the leader of the pack wasn't having it. Sarah lived in Inglewood and wore her long black hair styled tightly half up / half down, crunchy with hair gel. She smiled a lot but with a look in her eye that warned she might be seconds away from sucker punching you. I was both fascinated by and terrified of her.

"Raise your hand if you want her to sit with us," she said to the girls lounging on the concrete steps. She didn't take her eyes off me when she said it, smirking the whole time.

Not one person raised their hand.

"See? No one wants you here," she said, waving her arms around dramatically. "So *leave.*"

My knees wanted to buckle, but I made it to the girls' bathroom and locked myself in one of the stalls for the rest of the lunch period. After that, I spent most of my lunchtimes in the stalls, lifting my feet whenever someone came in so that they wouldn't recognize my tennis shoes. The smell of urine on concrete made it hard to eat, but it was better than risking running into Sarah in an empty hallway. I was on her radar now.

Over the next few months, she pulled out strands of my hair during class, chanted names at me in the yard with some of the other girls, and stole my Starter jacket. But I still wanted to be part of her crew. That's how inextricably linked I thought their approval was to my identity as a Latina.

Fortunately, it was only a matter of patiently biding my time. By the end of freshman year, Sarah was expelled, and without her looming influence, I started sophomore year having convinced the crew of Latinas to accept me as their homegirl. I was in—eating lunch every day on the steps I'd previously been voted off of, passing paper notes written in Old English handwriting back and forth between classes, lining up in two rows to take group photos at our school dances, and sitting in the stands together to watch the hot upperclassmen play football. My new friend Gabriela even had a hookup for me—a guy in the same gang as her boyfriend. "He's the gangster with a heart of gold," she said, as if she had to sell me on the idea. It was the last rite of passage to cement my status. A high school version of an arranged marriage.

They called him Spider.

Some said it was because he was hard to catch, and others said it was because when there was trouble, he was the first to disappear. Gabriela thought we'd make a good couple because he had green eyes and liked "good girls." But I didn't need any convincing. I had wanted to date a gangster ever since my days at Virginia Park. Someone to cruise with on the weekends or to write me letters from jail, with the names of lowrider oldies scribbled in the margin. Maybe he'd call legendary radio DJ Art Laboe and make a Sunday Night Oldies dedication. "The Agony and the Ecstasy" or "I'm Your Puppet" or "Confessin' a Feeling."

Gabriela and I made plans to meet up with Spider and his friends on the Santa Monica Pier on a Friday night around ten. I wore my best outfit—size 40 burgundy jeans, a tight white bodysuit, a black wooden cross necklace, and brown lipstick, leaving my hair loose down to my lower back, because my mom always told me it looked better that way.

We waited around in front of an empty arcade, as the high-pitched sounds of Skee-Ball lanes and video games running on autopilot filled the air. And then I saw them in the distance. Strutting in lockstep toward us. They couldn't have been more than fifteen or sixteen years old, but in my eyes, they were hardest guys I'd ever seen. Their 1990s Westside gangster uniform was impeccable—white T-shirts, pressed Dickies, and buffed Cortez.

And then my jaw dropped. It was him. *Him* him. I was

sure of it. The stocky guy I had locked eyes with two summers before at Virginia Park. The guy I had spent months
scanning picnic benches, freeway overpasses, and house
parties for. I had filled entire sections of my diary with daydreams about who he might be. Yet now, only a few feet
away, I could see what I had previously missed. His shy
smile, hypnotizing green eyes, and a raised, jagged scar on
his forehead.

"Hey...what up?" he said. His voice had a deep rasp to
it, like tires over gravel. It didn't match his teenage body.
"You wanna go for a walk or something?"

The Santa Monica Pier was deserted at that hour, with
all the street performers and tourists gone. We found a solitary picnic table at the end of the dark pier, and Spider sat
on top of it, turning me around to face him and then pulling
me in between his legs, with the familiarity of a boyfriend.
All the worry I'd had that he wouldn't like me wafted away
with the scent of dead fish. I wanted to stop time right then
and there. Feeling the ocean breeze on that dirty bench,
wrapped in Spider's arms, was my definition of bliss. He
asked me a throwaway question—like "What's new?" or
"How's it going?"—but his eyes were laser-focused on my
mouth as I answered, trying my best to sound cool.

Oh my God, he's already gonna kiss me, I thought. All the
moves I had practiced in my bathroom mirror immediately
left my head, and I just closed my eyes and waited. When
his lips met mine, only the second kiss of my life, they were
warm and tasted sweet like candy (which I later learned
was Cisco). We made out on that bench until our eyes were
at half-mast and my hair looked like I'd teased it out with

Aqua Net. Spider seemed to relax after that and started to ask me real questions.

We talked about school (he had been kicked out) and where he lived (nowhere and everywhere). I told him I was trying out for the drill team and that my favorite subject was English. He smiled at me as I rambled on. No guy had ever looked at me like that before. Like he *really* liked me. I felt self-conscious all of a sudden.

"What's this from?" I asked, running my index finger over the uneven scar on his forehead to change the subject.

"Knife fight," he said, his full lips curling into a smirk.

"Oh." I tried my best to act both unalarmed and unimpressed. He stared at me for a few seconds, sizing me up with his emerald eyes.

"Nahhhhh, I'm just playing with you!" He broke out laughing. "I fell."

I knew better than to fully believe either story, but I also didn't care. When we walked back to our friends, Spider grabbed my hand and kept holding it in front of everyone. It was settled; I was his girl. Back at school on Monday, my social status was upgraded accordingly. Everyone wanted to hear how it went with Spider, and I couldn't have been happier to gush.

Our relationship felt like a series of secret moments, since he lived like a runaway—always on the street, with no one really paying attention. He stole a car—a G-ride—to take me out on our second date, a gesture I found to be incredibly romantic. He was thoughtful, buying Jack Daniel's coolers just for me when we'd go to the beach at night to drink with his boys, knowing how much I hated 40s. He'd play me lowrider oldies over the phone, making a point to turn up Delegation's "Oh Honey" (a cue I took to mean that it was our song). He even came over to our apartment to watch MTV with me.

"Niiiice! I just saw you live off of *High*land Street." He chuckled, striding inside.

I didn't get it.

"Never mind," he said, shaking his head. I could tell he thought it was cute that I had no idea what he was talking about.

How my mom didn't put two and two together that the kid throwing up gang signs to the beat of Dre's "Keep Their Heads Ringin'" in her living room *might* be in a gang is still a mystery. But by the spring of my sophomore year, her depression had lifted and she was busy chasing a toddler around, so I was mostly on my own. Which is how one afternoon, I ended up snuggled up with Spider in the back room of a drug dealer's crash pad.

We had left our friends partying in the living room to find a make-out spot. The small bedroom we locked ourselves into had nothing more than a bed, a mismatched dresser, and piles of musty clothes strewn around. As we kissed on top of someone's dirty laundry, I started worrying about my nonexistent curves. It was something I didn't like about myself. But then I figured, if a guy like Spider wanted me, then I must be desirable, just like the girls in the park.

And there was something else. I truly felt safe in his arms. Someone had my back now and would protect me at all costs. Someone with access to a gun.

As Spider's hands drifted to the button on my jeans, I squirmed away and looked him in the eyes. There was a ray of sunlight streaming through the curtains, illuminating his face.

"Why did you get jumped in?" I asked, essentially killing the mood.

His face became serious. He exhaled loudly and told me about being an eleven-year-old kid waiting around Virginia Park for his parents to get off work until it was dark outside. Cold, hungry, and alone. The guys in the gang started looking after him and became his family.

I listened to him put into words what it felt like to be a kid who was forgotten and what a relief it was to feel like he belonged somewhere. As he talked, his eyes welled up, and heat surged in my chest. I was sure it was love. We were the same, he and I; at our core, both of us were hurt kids searching for belonging. And I was the *one* person he was letting in to see the real him. It was meant to be. We would save each other.

But as the weeks passed, the time between his calls started to grow longer. I had no way to reach Spider other than to page him and wait by the phone for his call back. I made a habit of keeping my black pager within eyesight during the school day and of sleeping with it right next to my pillow. When he called, I was ecstatic; when he didn't, I was miserable. Up and down. Hot and cold.

I didn't recognize it at the time, but the unpredictability of our relationship triggered my layered childhood memories of instability. I was sure that I was on the verge of being abandoned. I never knew when he'd show up, when he'd call, or where I stood. The truth was that he did whatever he felt like doing, whenever he felt like it. Just like my father.

For months, I waited for him to ask me out on a date again or at least call consistently, hoping he'd go back to how he was in the beginning. Yet the torture of waiting around for him grew to be too much. Maybe if I'd grown up in a less unstable household, I would've been turned off by the whole thing, but instead I was thrown into anxious thoughts and sleeplessness. I'd call Alma for marathon phone calls, where we'd deconstruct every detail of what he'd said, what I'd said, and what it all had meant. Spider was all we seemed to talk about, and even *I* was getting sick of listening to myself drone on. Desperate to get off the roller coaster and, frankly, out of exhaustion, I decided to break up with him.

When we met up at the park and the words left my mouth, the crushed look on his face was the confirmation of his feelings that I had long been hoping for. I immediately regretted what I'd done. Turns out, he *did* care.

Unfortunately, it was too late. His face suddenly went cold.

"All right," Spider said, turning on his heel to leave.

"It's just that I felt—"

"Nah, I'm good," he said, holding up his hand to stop me from saying more. "You take care."

As I watched him walk back toward the benches where I'd first spotted him, I felt so stupid. And I felt *worse* than I had before. He was now more out of my reach than ever. My stomach twisted itself into an even tighter knot. What was I thinking?

Spider actively avoided me after that, no matter how hard I tried to see him again. I wanted to take back everything I'd said, but he wouldn't give me a chance to. I paged him, I showed up at the park, I went to parties he was likely to be at—and nothing. The finality of our breakup tormented me, and the feeling was only compounded by how seemingly blasé he was whenever Gabriela and the girls would see him out.

The confusing part was that the more pain and trouble I found myself in, the higher my grades seemed to go at school. It felt like some sort of twisted reward system. I understand now that extreme perfectionism and compartmentalization were some of my most reliable coping mechanisms. Being busy was how I avoided myself. Like Sunny & the Sunliners said, "Smile Now, Cry Later."

After Spider disappeared from my life, I started gobbling up accomplishments like I was some kind of ravenous Ms. Pac-Man. The busier I was, the less anxious and more in control I felt. I became the captain of the drill team, class president, and a campus minister. I joined the school choir and the math club. All the while taking AP classes and earning straight A's. I still hung out with my same group of friends—going to kickbacks with whichever cholos they were dating and sneaking into clubs in Hollywood—but at the same time, I had ditched the size 40 pants and was auditioning to sing Gershwin in the school musical.

And it worked. My memories of Spider gradually became a dull ache in the background of a crowded calendar. I even started going out on dates with other guys. But I still scanned the park for him whenever I passed it and looked for his tagging on freeway overpasses.

When I was cast as the female lead in the spring musical *Crazy for You* during my junior year, I was relieved to throw myself into a rehearsal schedule that would keep my mind occupied every day after school and on weekends. After years of acting and playwriting with VAP, the theater felt like a safe space to me. But my Broadway dreams were short-lived. Soon after rehearsals started, Abi was diagnosed with breast cancer.

Even though I had been a distracted teenager ever since I started high school, Abi was still my everything. My second mother, my pillow, and the one whose love I felt the most. For my quinceañera the year before, she had actually hired a mariachi trio to sing "Las Mañanitas" under my bedroom window at dawn. I took for granted she'd always be there—our entire family did. None of us had a clue that Abi had been holding on to a secret. She had found a lump in one of her breasts but was too scared to tell anyone, so she just stopped touching it and tried to ignore that it was there.

Cancer was her absolute deepest fear. Abi's mother had died from metastasized breast cancer, and in her eyes, a diagnosis was as good as a death sentence. Besides, she didn't want to burden anyone in our family with her medical bills. By the time the lump grew too big to ignore and Abi finally went to see a doctor, the cancer had spread throughout her body.

I watched in horror as, over the course of just a few months of play rehearsals, my pudgy grandmother withered down to skin and bones, lost all of her hair, and only had the energy to lie in a hospital bed we set up in her living room. Seeing her crumpled in that bed, crying with her hands over her face, was the new low point of my life. She was my closest companion, but this time there was nothing I could do to take away her suffering.

On one of the final days she could gather enough strength to leave the house, Abi visited a local church, bought a powder-blue rosary, and asked the priest to pray a blessing over it. When she called me to her bedside days later and placed it in my palm, I could feel that the rosary beads carried with them her hope, faith, light, and love, like in the novenas of my childhood. She raised a frail arm and made the sign of the cross on my forehead. It was the last gift—of so many—she gave me. I leaned down to kiss her soft, sunken cheek and told her that I loved her, making the sign of the cross on her forehead. I wish I'd told her a million more times.

Abi died the morning of the show's opening night. My mom, Monica, and I drove in silence to visit her still-warm body. We were too overcome with grief to cry, afraid that letting even a few tears out would break open the dam and drown us all. Then I went to school like normal, so I'd be able to perform in the play and not let anyone down.

Opening night was a blur. I had to check out of my body to make it through. Splinter myself off from everything I was feeling. It was the only way I could dance onstage with jazz hands, singing "I Got Rhythm," twelve hours after seeing Abi for the very last time.

When I started senior year, there was a part of me that stayed fragmented, that never checked back in. I won homecoming queen in the fall, and as I stood in the middle of the football field in a white floor-length dress with white roses in my hair and a crown on my head, I wondered why I didn't feel anything. Why didn't I feel happy? I smiled, waved, and posed for photos, but inside I felt fractured. Split between what I was projecting on the outside and how I was feeling on the inside. I had now purposely separated the two so many times before, I couldn't recognize which feelings were real. Besides, I actually thought it was noble to put my experience second. To take the back seat in my own life.

With Abi gone, my anxiety became worse than ever. The now-constant agitation I was feeling made me afraid to be far from home. I had never seen a therapist or heard the terms *panic disorder* or *anxiety attack*. I know now that high school—specifically age fourteen—is the average time of onset for all mental health issues. But back then, I assumed I was either losing my mind or about to have a stroke. What would I do, I wondered, if my heart started racing again and I was far from home or couldn't reach my mom?

I began to look for ways to make my world small and guarded. If I had a date, I'd suggest that we rent a movie at Blockbuster so I wouldn't have to leave the house. I started isolating myself and sabotaging my friendships. And when the time came to apply to college, I applied to only three—all within twenty miles of our apartment. But in truth, my limited applications weren't only because of my anxiety; my mom and I simply didn't know any better.

I wish I could say that applying to college was a time made up of campus visits and anticipation, but the whole thing was mostly confusing and obscure. My mom and I filled out paper applications by hand, and I worked on the essays on my own. As is the case for many First and Onlys, there were no encouraging academic counselors illuminating the way, family members sharing application tips, or college tours. My mom was still taking classes toward getting her *own* degree, and I don't think my father ever went to college. I figured I had a decent shot because of my grades, but what did I know.

When a letter from USC arrived in the mail and it was in a large, thick envelope, I tore it open with relief more than anything. In my trembling hands was the key to the "bright future" everyone had been pointing me toward since I was a kid. My family may have had a limited understanding of how higher education works, but like many immigrant parents, they were adamant that college was *the* gateway to the American Dream. And somehow, I had pulled it off—in the midst of losing Abi and with my anxiety spinning out of control. I was going to college.

My mom told anyone who would listen that her daughter would be attending USC. Seeing her beam as she shared the news with her hairdresser, our neighbor, and the mailman made it feel like the achievement was bigger than just me. It was as if my mom were going too—and Abi, and even Abito. Yet in her enthusiasm to inform the masses, my mom had a bad idea with good intentions. She called my father and invited him to fly in for my graduation.

The day started off as expected—I sat in Saint Monica's

Church with my classmates, wearing a gold cap and gown, and went onstage to receive the principal's award for academic achievement. And then my father showed up—accompanied by an older brother of mine I didn't know I had.

Apparently, my brother—also a Campoverdi and a couple of years older than I was—had been put up for adoption as a baby, but my father had recently tracked him down and decided to bring him to my graduation as a big surprise. It was a surprise all right. So much so that I sat crying on the curb as my classmates drove away on a school bus to Disneyland for Grad Nite.

It was all too much to process—seeing my father for only the third time in my life, plus the bombshell news of a sibling, on a day that was supposed to be about signing yearbooks and cutting cake. As for my newfound brother? He let me know the very next day that he wanted nothing to do with either of us.

As I stared down USC, I hit my tipping point. The pressure I felt—to be a perfect student, the quintessential Latina, dutiful daughter, family hero—was staggering. The exhaustion of continuously balancing all sides had run over. I needed a lifeline. I needed the identity and the armor that I had relied on to get me through the early days of high school. I needed Spider.

I'd had other boyfriends since we broke up, but I'd never forgotten the way I felt around him—invulnerable and unafraid. If I was going to be able to hold on to my past, and to my nerve, while careening into the future, I had to recapture that part of myself again. The fearless side.

When I heard Spider might be at a certain graduation party in Santa Monica, I showed up with one purpose only: to get him back. Honors student attends private university with gangster dropout boyfriend by her side. It was an unlikely fantasy, but it was mine all the same.

The second he walked in the door, I took off across the dance floor in a beeline toward the eighteen-year-old I was convinced was the answer to all my problems.

"Hi. Can I talk to you outside, please?" I said a bit too intensely as he took a swig of his Corona. We hadn't seen each other in two years, but this time, I wouldn't let the opportunity pass me by.

He nodded and followed me out to the back alley, his baggy pants dragging on the stained cement and broken glass.

I immediately dove into apologizing for breaking up with him. And then I blurted out that I loved him, asked if we could try again, and held my breath for the longest ten seconds of my life.

"I love you too," he finally said, cracking that playful smile I adored. "Okay, let's do it."

Calm flooded my body as he kissed me next to the dumpster. The trash heap might as well have been the Eiffel Tower as I inhaled his aroma of Cool Water cologne mixed with cigarettes. Everything seemed that perfect. I had my love and my protector back, and he had told me he loved me. For the very. First. Time.

When we returned to the party minutes later, he promised to call me the next day, and for once, I believed him.

But he never called.

As the days went by, I stared at the phone, willing it to ring, just as I had two years earlier. I couldn't believe that he had the nerve to treat me so badly again, especially after what we'd said to each other in the alley.

I supposed it could be argued that he had a pretty good excuse. Alma called me after about a week to tell me what she'd heard around the streets: Apparently, when Spider and his homeboys left the graduation party that night, there was a shooting and they had all been arrested. Spider was in jail.

I spent the weekend crying in my room, listening to "Oh Honey" on repeat. Even though I was sure that he was innocent, I understood how street politics worked. Spider would be heading to prison soon. They would all go down together.

But I was wrong. By the time I heard the news that Spider had sold out his friends to the police, he had vanished into the depths of the witness protection program. All of his former best friends were now his mortal enemies, and they were searching for him, but I knew no one would ever find him again. Including me. He was gone for good this time. As was everything that came along with him. Love, security, validation, and protection. I'd never see or hear from him again. I was on my own.

Just weeks away from starting college, my sense of who I was remained more polarized than ever. I wanted Spider, and I wanted USC. I was proud of my Latina identity, and I was diving headfirst into doing supposed "white people things." I wanted to relate to my friends and family at home, and I wanted to sit in rooms with CEOs and presidents. Of course, none of these things were mutually exclusive, but I still thought I had to deplete myself to find the perfect balance. Lean too far one way and I'd be a sellout. Lean too far the other way and I'd be an outsider. My life felt like it was being advanced simultaneously on parallel tracks that were destined to collide.

These types of dizzying dichotomies make up the Bicultural Balancing Act that many First and Onlys face. Whether based on race, class, or another social group, alternating between seemingly contradictory expectations and behavior patterns is common. It's also tricky and emotionally exhausting.

As First and Onlys, we have dual citizenship to worlds that often appear at odds with each other. We often walk multiple tightropes at the same time, with little attention given to how this dynamic can affect our mental health. Beyond code-switching, it's social-identity-switching. And there's an additional toll associated with contorting to fit in depending on the social context, no matter how seamlessly one is able to manage it. And that is: When we've learned to survive by alternating between different selves, how do we ever know for sure what our *authentic* identity is?

My high school experience was defined by a Bicultural Balancing Act, and to the naked eye, I nailed it. I was one of a small number of graduates from my high school heading to a private university. One of the kids who'd "made it." But who was I really? The wannabe chola, the overachiever, or a little bit of both? I was about to learn what happens when your sense of self is obscured by how good you are at morphing to survive, and in the most unforgiving of places: a university with traditions as old as its history.

CHAPTER FIVE

CRASH INTO ME

USC WAS IN full bloom in August of 1997—cardinal and gold draped on every building, flowering hedge, and human body, as far as the eye could see. It was a perfect, warm, and desert-dry California morning, and Alumni Park was vibrating, thanks to the Trojan Marching Band. Despite growing up in the same city, I had never set foot on campus before or heard the iconic fight song, but the pounding drums and climbing horn sequences contributed to the growing certainty in my gut that something life-altering was about to happen. As a seventeen-year-old incoming freshman, I wasn't just starting college; I was starting college in a movie.

The closest I'd come to experiencing a campus like USC's was watching the 1970 film *Love Story* with my mom. She idealized the cross-class romance so much she started calling me Ali as a kid (after the lead actress Ali McGraw) and had me play the film's theme song on the piano at her wedding to Mario. Even though I wasn't at Harvard, like in *Love Story*, the brick buildings and tree-lined winding pathways surrounding me might as well have been in Cambridge. USC had the same storybook collegiate ideal. Yet I wasn't wearing a preppy peacoat and turtleneck like Ali. I was in my favorite gray ribbed dress from Forever 21 and towering Steve Madden cork platforms, lips stained chola brown.

Unfortunately, my movie's plot was about to take a hard left turn. By midday during freshman orientation, whispers were snaking around campus: "Did you hear that some anorexic-looking girl fainted? Probably from starving herself."

I raised my eyebrows like everyone else, feigning disbelief and joining them in trying to guess the identity of the unfortunate girl.

But it was me. I had been that girl.

Three hours earlier, in the historic Bovard Auditorium—where Martin Luther King Jr. had once spoken and over a thousand members of the incoming class of 2001 had gathered for the president's welcome—panic had lifted me out of my seat. It shoved me out the double doors, through Romanesque archways, and down the concrete front stairs.

By the time high-pitched ringing started flooding my ears and everything started to spin, I had just reached USC's iconic Tommy Trojan statue—smack in the center of campus. My knees gave out as the world went black, and I hit the ground hard in the shadow of the school mascot.

When I regained consciousness, I was mortified to be lying on the ground, with strangers hovering over my body—not to mention, petrified that my anxiety was already sabotaging this new phase of my life. Why did I collapse when I was exactly where I had worked so hard to be? According to my mom, a degree from USC meant I would be able to earn "good money." I had family members who couldn't afford to buy a car, who worked crazy hours for minimum wage, and who couldn't afford health insurance. How could I blow this opportunity on the very first day?

Moments earlier in Bovard, the precariousness of my newfound social status had made me feel physically trapped. In my actual seat. My brain was telling me that the only way I could make anything of myself and, more immediately, the only way I could claw my way out of my family's paycheck-to-paycheck existence was to sit in that very chair and not move a muscle. And keep not moving for the next four years. Claustrophobia clamped down on me like handcuffs until all I could think of to do was run.

After I came to, someone pulled my mom out of parents' orientation, and she rushed to the campus health center with my sister Monica, who was fast asleep in a neon-pink jogging stroller. The doctor found nothing physically wrong with me, suggested I see a therapist on campus, and sent me on my way with a prescription for Xanax every four to six hours. The fact that I was so easily given highly addictive benzodiazepines with no supervision as a seventeen-year-old seems ludicrous to me now. But, then again, so does the idea of trying to regain my emotional equilibrium by rushing a sorority in one of the most notorious Greek systems in the country.

Sitting on a bench in the center of campus about to

take my first Xanax, I could tell that my mom was deep in damage-control mode.

"Look at all the friends you'll make!" she said, holding up a photo of a hundred mostly blond white women posed with their hands on their knees in front of a mansion. The glossy brochure had the words *Sorority Rush* and *Sisterhood* splashed across it in cursive.

"I think it's like a club or something. You *need* to do this," she insisted. I could tell she was worried about me by how hard she was trying to sell the idea (and by the sign of the cross she had just made on my forehead). Neither of us had the faintest clue what a sorority was.

I swallowed one of the pink oval pills as I considered my options, feeling an odd tingly heaviness quickly take over my body as the minutes passed. I had stayed far away from drugs in high school, but now I didn't feel like I had a choice. It was either that or have another panic attack in front of my new classmates, and I couldn't risk that ever happening again.

To make matters worse, my mom had turned down the on-campus housing that had been included in my admissions packet—thinking dorms were just for international students. I was stuck commuting twenty-eight miles to and from school every day in a silver Mercury Capri we bought for $2,000 with my mom's earned-income tax credit refund. The miserable death trap had no heat or AC and played only one staticky station on the AM dial—Radio Disney. There would be no safe haven for me on campus and no new friends from the dorms. As I imagined how freshman year was likely to pan out, even the Xanax wasn't enough to keep my heart from racing. The possibility that, after all I'd been through, I might not last a week in college was terrifying enough to push me into action.

Which is why days later, I joined hundreds of freshman women in a sweaty single-file line down the two residential blocks that held all of the sorority and fraternity houses at USC—a.k.a. the Row. But they weren't really houses. They were dollhouse-looking mansions, with manicured lawns accented by colorful blooms and the occasional Roman column. At least the sororities were. The fraternities had empty kegs and red Solo cups on their lawns, rather than roses and tulips. But the worst fraternity on the Row was still larger than the apartment building I grew up in.

Pledging a sorority seemed straightforward enough. As rushees, our job was to visit each house over the course of a week for one-on-one chats with our potential sorority sisters, usually over flavored iced tea or spa water. At the end of the week, a "mutual selection process" would take place, and we'd be matched based on reciprocated interest.

Or not. That was the nightmare scenario—to have your friendship categorically rejected by thousands of women before the first day of class. Would this be a shameful replay of having my friendship voted down by the cholas in high school?

The dress code for rush was "nice casual," which apparently meant something very different depending on where you came from. Next to my fresh-faced pastel-sundress-wearing fellow hopefuls, I looked like I'd just stumbled out of a nightclub. I was wearing gold hoops, red lipstick, and head-to-toe black when my cohort approached our first sorority house, a two-story white Victorian manor.

"Okay, ladies, over here," the rush counselor said, motioning for all of us to huddle in front of the entrance. I peeked at the other freshman girls at my side, eyes fixed on the doorway with palpable excitement, and realized that they'd likely been planning for this moment for a long time.

Suddenly, the painted wooden door flung open, revealing a mass of bouncing blond heads. They were chanting a welcome song in the cadence of a pep squad cheer: *"We'll do anything for you, anything you want us to!"* Noticing that the women around me were enthusiastically clapping along with the beat, I joined in. *This is so weird,* I thought. But if I could come out on the other side with friends and a safe house near campus, it would 100 percent be worth it.

When the song ended and the doorway cleared, the women around me began to march right into the house, but I hesitated. I wasn't sure I was ready to cross that threshold. From then on, I would be stepping into a different crowd—scrambling up a crooked ladder into a new social class. One that had a defined lifestyle, frames of reference, behaviors, and traits that I didn't relate to. Before, poverty was a gauge of legitimacy and authenticity. In this world, wealth was.

When I eventually stepped into the spacious gardenia-scented foyer, the soundtrack to my life abruptly switched from Dr. Dre to Dave Matthews Band. I was escorted to a side living room, where I was seated knee to knee with a petite blonde wearing large diamond stud earrings.

"Where you from?" she chirped, cocking her head as if to better size me up. I was used to hearing that question asked for a different purpose—to suss out a rival's gang affiliation.

I remembered my mom's instructions: "When they ask where you're from, say Beverly Hills, because you were born at Cedars-Sinai hospital. That's *in* Beverly Hills, so you are technically *from* Beverly Hills." Her heart was in the right place, but the message was obvious. Being myself wouldn't be enough at USC.

I don't know who looked less convinced of my adopted hometown—me or my interviewer.

And then came the question that to this day still makes me wince: "What does your daddy do?" I told her that my father was an entrepreneur, which rolled off the tongue easier than "womanizing grifter." I also quickly learned to stop asking each sorority if they offered financial aid, after the first few blank stares.

As rush week dragged on, the houses, women, and promises of lifelong sisterhood all bled into one Laura Ashley–themed version of the Hunger Games. Each day, the sororities pruned their lists based on the previous day's conversations, and our cohort's numbers rapidly diminished. Each night, my fellow rushees went back to their newly decorated dorms while I drove back down the 10 to the apartment I shared with my mom and Monica.

I was simultaneously repulsed by the Greek system and desperate to be chosen. And by some miracle, at the end of the week I was handed an envelope with a cardstock note inside that read *Delta Delta Delta*. I was in.

When I put on my blue sweatshirt that had three large triangles sewn onto the front, it felt like I'd been offered a seat at the university-wide cool kids' table. In case there's any question as to what USC's Greek system was like in the early 2000s, *Legally Blonde* was filmed on our campus while I was there, and my sorority's group photo was used as a movie prop in Elle Woods's sorority house.

In the weeks that followed, I scrambled to figure out who Jimmy Buffett was and to incorporate the word *stoked* into my vocabulary. I technically looked the part, after buying knockoff plaid Abercrombie shorts and Reef flip-flops, and replacing my brown lipstick with clear lip gloss. But I knew better than to relax into this new persona. I'd already learned the hard way that fortunes and futures could change overnight, in either direction.

Social mobility is like the children's board game Chutes and Ladders. If you're lucky enough to land on a "good deed," you climb the proverbial social ladder at a meteoric speed. If you accidentally land on the "wrong spot," you backslide down a chute so fast your head will spin. It's tricky to navigate the fragility of a sudden new social status, yet First and Onlys often confront Chutes and climb Social Ladders for decades. Not because we're clout chasers or status-obsessed but because in order to create financial stability and economic mobility for ourselves and our families, First and Onlys *must* transcend the social class we were born into. One isn't possible without the other.

USC was my first big social ladder. It was when I had no choice but to coexist within disparate social classes for the very first time, and when those two sets of circumstances were just one blurry summer apart. Even as a student, the Chutes and Social Ladders kept coming at me in a hurry, and many ladders seemed to have a corresponding chute hiding right around the corner. In this case, the campus club fair.

It was midfall, and there were dozens of booths strewn around the middle of campus, each announcing its respective club in bubble letters on colorful butcher paper. I was riding a beat-up beach cruiser on my way back to campus from the sorority house, where I'd just eaten lunch for free (by far my favorite perk of being a pledge), when I spotted the words *Latina* and *Mexican*. I parked my bike and walked toward the signs. Whatever the club was, I wanted to be a part of it.

I approached the booth with a smile, but the two young Latinas staffing the table looked up at me suspiciously.

"What does this club do?" I asked the girl in front of me. She was wearing a ponytail and large gold hoops. I had identical ones in my closet and was about to tell her that when she said, "Yeah, so…if you've done *that*, then you can't do *this*."

She nodded toward my chest.

I looked down at my T-shirt, confused, but then I followed her line of vision directly to my sorority pledge pin. As a new pledge, I was required to wear a small enamel Tri Delt pin at all times until initiation.

Caught off guard, I considered how to respond, but

before I could say anything, she explained more emphatically this time.

"You can't *be*...I mean, *do* both." And then she turned back to her notebook.

The absurdity of the idea that I had instantly forfeited the right to my Brownness by joining a sorority was not lost on me. In truth, the Greek system made me more aware of my Latinidad on a daily basis than ever before. When you're Brown in a predominantly white environment, your otherness tends to be mirrored back to you more often than not.

Spring of freshman year, I was at a party at one of the best fraternity houses when an upperclassman walked over to me. He was from Newport Beach and looked like a surfer straight out of Central Casting. When he wasn't surfing, he was riding around campus on his skateboard, honey-colored curls blowing into his eyes. Everyone was watching us talk, and I was beside myself to be the center of his attention for a minute. And then he asked about my plans for the week.

"Hey, Cinco de Mayo is coming up! Is your family, like, having a *fiesta*?"

I had no idea if he was making fun of me, so I didn't respond.

He continued, "You know, like, with a *piñata*? And *tacos*?"

His eyes were childlike, and I realized that he was just honestly curious, albeit in the most cringey, stereotype-laden way. He continued by telling me I was "exotic," and I suppose in his world, I truly was. In high school, I had been teased for "acting like a white girl" because of my grades, but now at USC, I had somehow become a "spicy Latina" overnight.

If there was a total-immersion program for Greek life, though, it was the experience of moving into the house sophomore year. My living conditions leveled up big-time. Built in 1897, the three-story Tri Delt mansion could house up to sixty-five girls at once and had three (!) living rooms filled with elegant upholstered furniture, multiple fireplaces, several full-time chefs, and a twenty-four-hour security detail.

I'd never felt more rich or more poor in my life. Even my sister Monica—now four years old—was spellbound when she came to visit, running up and down the hallways, poking her head into what felt like a never-ending line of bedrooms. Every morning, I'd walk down our winding mahogany staircase in my fluffy robe to the breakfast room, where stacks of newspapers and steamy fresh blueberry muffins were waiting like a dream.

It blew my mind that the trash can in my bedroom was miraculously empty by the time I made it back upstairs. Yet it wasn't magic. My trash was being emptied by our Mexican housekeepers and the daily made-to-order omelets were prepared by our Black cook. I made a point to get to know the staff that worked at the house and spoke Spanish to the housekeepers. Even so, it was jarring to be a woman of color in a predominantly white environment, who was being waited on by women of color. At times, I identified more with our household staff than with my own sorority sisters. I had way more in common with them in terms of background and life experience. It was like being a social-class double agent.

And then there were the reality checks that came at the most unfortunate times. For winter formal my junior year, I invited a senior who I had a huge crush on to be my date. I wanted every detail to be flawless—from the gold dress I snagged on sale to my manicured nails. Since I didn't own any jewelry other than cheap trinkets from Claire's, my mom had gifted me a solitaire diamond ring that once belonged to my great-grandmother. As my date and I sat at a table drinking martinis with another couple, I was finally starting to relax when my ring caught his eye.

"Whoa! Let me see that." He laughed, grabbing my hand and pulling it up to his face to inspect it further. "That's the *smallest* diamond I've ever seen in my whole life! Look, isn't that the smallest diamond you've *ever* seen?"

He dragged my hand in front of my sorority sister and her date, and they joined him in laughter. I didn't know what else to do but to smile along with them, as if it didn't bother me. But when my date wasn't paying attention, I turned the band around so that the mini diamond was hidden from sight for the rest of the night.

By the time Tri Delt's annual mother-daughter tea came around junior year, I knew to be on guard. Held in an ornate ballroom at the Ritz-Carlton hotel bordering San Marino—a wealthy suburb east of Downtown LA, named one of "America's Richest Places"—it was a medley of mothers in St. John suits, pastel rose centerpieces, and delicately cut finger sandwiches.

"I know what I'll wear," my mom said the morning

of the tea as she dug through the back of her closet, past Skittles-colored dresses with fringe and spaghetti straps. She laid out a demure beige sheath dress on the bed. "It's perfect. Boring and expensive-looking!"

My mom had never been to the Ritz or attended high tea, but she didn't have an ounce of self-consciousness about her. She had embodied act-like-you've-been-there-before energy for as long as I could remember. It came in handy when she had started taking classes at Santa Monica Community College with only an elementary school education, and I saw it on full display as she put on the gold and pearl jewelry from her wedding day that she kept hidden in the back of her drawer, for only the most special of occasions. She could finesse any environment because she sincerely believed she had a right to be there. It was her superpower.

As a child, whenever we'd be stopped at a red light next to a shiny Porsche or a Mercedes convertible, she'd turn to me and say, "We'd look *so* much better in that car!" I'd roll my eyes, but there was something about her confidence that kept me from feeling undeserving.

I see now that my mom unintentionally taught me to hurl myself at the unfamiliar with an expectation of admittance. Maybe not acceptance per se, but access all the same. And wasn't that close enough?

The day of the event, we drove to the Ritz in her Honda, with its loud rumbling engine and its passenger-side window that was permanently stuck halfway open.

"Remember to put your napkin in your lap as soon as we sit down, okay?" I told her.

"Yes, I know how to act, *Mom*," she teased me.

There was no street parking on the massive palm-tree-lined boulevard, so we pulled into the valet line, idling behind Range Rovers and BMWs. But I knew we wouldn't stay long.

When I was growing up, there were certain extravagances that were considered off-limits. When we went out to eat—which was rare—we never ordered drinks, because they added too much to the bill. Only water. And we never, *ever* used valet parking. There was always street parking to be found, and if that meant you had to walk a bit, well, then you'd get a little bonus exercise.

"Fifteen dollars! There's no way," my mom huffed, peeling out of the valet line noisily.

She drove down an alleyway alongside the hotel, next to the service entrance and trash bins. There were florist vans along the far wall, where uniformed Latino workers were unloading flower arrangements that were likely for our tea party. As she made a U-turn and parked behind one of the vans under an AUTHORIZED VEHICLES ONLY sign, I gave her a *You must be kidding me* look.

"What? Let's go," she said, slipping on her pastel-pink wedding heels.

Over the next two hours, we drank herbal tea out of dainty china, ate buttery scones, and posed cheek to cheek for the professional photographer making the rounds to each table. I glanced over at my mom throughout the afternoon and felt proud, watching her make small talk with the other moms effortlessly. We didn't seem like impostors; we seemed to fit in just like everyone else.

When the tea ended, we walked through the hotel

lobby with a mass of moms and daughters toward the valet. And then I remembered—our car was parked by the dumpster. As the crowd veered left to the valet line, my mom grabbed my arm and we made a hard right out the front double doors toward the alley.

Please don't be watching us, I silently mouthed. I turned around to see if anyone had noticed, but luckily, we had slipped away unseen. The ground under our heels abruptly switched from marble to gravel as we teetered farther and farther away from the other moms and daughters. People say you shouldn't forget where you come from, yet in my experience, where you come from never *lets* you forget.

Senior year, I was named social development chair of Tri Delt, which meant it was my job to make sure that my sisters "behaved properly" in public and represented our house "in a good light." If they didn't, I handed out punishments, like serving as the designated "sober sister" at parties. It was also up to me to teach a dining etiquette seminar to the entire sorority. When the moment came, I stood in front of a hundred girls in our chandeliered dining room and explained the difference between the American and European dining styles like I was Emily Post.

It felt like we were in Backwards Land. Here I was, a financial-aid kid, and I was the one teaching formal table manners to my sorority sisters. Manners that I was confident they'd have a chance to use at fancy restaurants in the future. As for me, I wasn't so sure. But either way, I was prepared, thanks to Abi.

Just as my mom's boldness had persuaded me to grasp at every opportunity, Abi's fascination with decorum and good manners had taught me how to behave once I'd arrived. One day after school when I was in second grade, Abi called me over to our round wooden dining room table. She was thumbing through a hardcover book with a faded blue spine and yellowing pages.

Motioning for me to jump onto her lap, she asked, "Do you know what dining etiquette is?" I shook my head.

She set two cloth place mats and silver utensils on opposite sides of the table.

"Let's practice, Alejandrita." Abi pointed to a small fork to the left of a larger fork, both on the left side of my plate. "What do you think this is for?" she asked. "The small one is for your salad. Since you eat salad first, that's the fork closest to your hand."

The rules didn't quite make sense, but I dutifully memorized them anyway, because I wanted to make Abi happy. How to eat bread properly (torn into pieces and buttered individually). Where to put my napkin when I went to the bathroom (on my seat) versus when I finished my meal (on the table). How to eat soup correctly (spooning away from myself).

I could tell Abi appreciated my enthusiasm. Manners and grace had always enthralled her; it was one of the reasons she was often tucked into the back of a movie theater as a teenager in Mexico. When Elizabeth Taylor or Rita Hayworth hit the screen, she'd memorize how they walked, how they held a glass, how they wore their hair, and the general way they carried themselves.

It was the reason why when I was a kid, she'd sometimes put me in one of my best dresses, take me out onto our balcony, and pin-curl my hair using bobby pins. Sitting in a beach chair next to a broken-down drying machine with Abi carefully twisting my hair into little brown tornados, I felt put-together and special. I wanted to be a lady, just like her (and Judy Garland).

We practiced for months until I could sit at a table with the Queen of England without flinching. By age nine, I knew the exact angle to set my knife down on the plate and the proper order of water and wineglasses. Abi said that if I made a habit of using formal etiquette at all times, it would soon become second nature and I'd always be prepared for any room or anyone. I took her words to heart.

Rather than make me feel self-conscious, learning dining etiquette as a child made me feel reassured and prepared. Even though we couldn't afford to go to restaurants very often, I could rehearse on my chilaquiles and pinto bean soup. And Abi was right; it did become force of habit.

If it seems like academics were secondary in my mind at the time, it's because they were. I knew how to be a good student. Studying, finals, grades—*that* I understood, or sure as hell would figure out. As is true for many First and Onlys and their parents, working hard was my default mode. In fact, the only thing that ever got me anywhere was working hard. Yet no amount of academic preparedness could make up for the general lack of acknowledgment around me that social-class backgrounds can affect the college experience in millions of ways that are microscopic but still wounding, like compounding paper cuts.

College highlighted social-class differences in ways

I wasn't prepared for. There was a hidden curriculum I'd missed that seemed to dictate everything from choosing dorms to buying books to navigating office hours. The syllabus included Sublime, Louis Vuitton purses, surfing, and the OC. Since I didn't have family who could help me make sense of the hurdles I was coming up against, I mostly kept my overwhelm to myself. It felt like I didn't have the right to complain anyway—to my family or to my friends back home. After all, I was the fortunate one who was at USC living in a mansion. *I'll just sound ungrateful*, I thought.

Why is it that a third of first-generation students drop out of college and 90 percent don't graduate on time? In part, it's because we are prepared for the classroom but rarely supported in our new lives outside of it. As I was experiencing firsthand, there are cultural norms that define college life—social network, beliefs, language, behavior, etiquette, frames of reference, clothing. And the prospect of social exclusion looms threateningly over all of it.

Many well-meaning pipeline programs for high-achieving first-generation students tend to concentrate their efforts on résumé writing and academics, missing a critical part of the equation. While removing structural barriers to college and career access is important, the social-class knowledge gap often goes unaddressed, an oversight that is all the more consequential given that one in three undergraduates now identifies as first-generation. It's a common cause of heightened stress for First and Onlys, and one that multiplied the level of anxiety I'd already been experiencing in high school.

When I ran out in the middle of a midterm exam freshman year, due to another panic attack—even after taking Xanax—I realized that if I was going to make it through college, I needed help. The therapist I'd seen on campus had scared me more than anything—grabbing a big leather book from his shelf and pointing to a section on agoraphobia. "Eventually, agoraphobics are unable to leave their house," it said. I left his office convinced I'd eventually be a recluse.

As a last resort, my mom turned to the Yellow Pages and searched under "anxiety therapists," finding a small ad that would change my life. Weeks later, I sat across a room from Lynne Freeman, a leading expert in anxiety treatment. I shared with her that I'd been making up excuses to drive to my sorority's date parties instead of taking the designated buses, since I had trouble riding in cars with other people. A recovering agoraphobic herself, she didn't look at me with pity or judgment, but with the kind eyes and compassion of someone who had been through it too. I started seeing her regularly, once a week. Our first order of business—getting me off Xanax. With her help, I stopped taking it by the end of freshman year, and thanks to the relaxation and breathing exercises she taught me, I finally had some tools to work with.

By sophomore year, with my anxiety under control, I was able to relax into just being a college student and hit my academic stride—devouring classes in ethnic and gender studies and supporting my thesis paper on Michel

Foucault's theory of the gaze by sitting in a glass box on Sunset Boulevard. I knew I wanted to tell stories for a living, but I hadn't been exposed to many professions, and I figured that the way to be a professional storyteller was to become a journalist. While studying at USC's Annenberg School for Communication and Journalism, I was determined to learn how to report on the people and the stories that were often overlooked, and first on my list were immigrants in LA. Ever since Prop 187, I'd paid attention to how immigration, and immigrants in general, was covered in news media. Bumper stickers at the time read SOS—SAVE OUR STATE, NO FUNDING ILLEGALS, promoting the idea that undocumented immigrants were drains on society. But as a child, I'd seen the complete opposite.

When Abi drove me to elementary school, each day we'd pass by the same scene in front of Home Depot in Santa Monica. Groups of undocumented immigrants waited on the sidewalk while men in full-sized pickup trucks pulled up to hire them for daylong construction jobs, paid in cash under the table. The years passed and I grew older, but the men and the pickup trucks stayed the same.

It was a simple scene from my childhood, but what I'd witnessed stuck with me. Whether in the fields, in the arts, in business, or in boardrooms, there was a big disconnect when it came to acknowledging the contributions immigrants make to our economy. I wanted to become the type of journalist who would have the courage to ask hard questions, challenge misperceptions, and write the truth. The plight of single mothers, the working poor, those without healthcare, the unhoused—I'd seen all of these issues up close, and there seemed to be a lot missing from the way they were being covered. I knew that if I could get my hands on a microphone, then I'd have the ability to pass the mic to others as well. I liked the idea of doing *that* for a living.

I ultimately found my way at USC, despite the rough start. I lived in the sorority house for three years, made some close friends, cheered in the Coliseum on Trojan football game days, and slow-danced to "Crash Into Me" at date parties with themes such as "Married to the Mob" and "Temptation Island." Even Monica got in on the fun, wearing a mini USC Song Girl uniform whenever she visited me, and sitting in on some of the etiquette lessons I taught. I felt proud to expose her to college, including sorority life, as an attainable reality.

Yet the closer graduation came, the more it began to feel that I'd been cosplaying a sorority girl in a temporary role that was soon to end. Reef sandals and Roxy shorts had been a costume—one that I had worn to fit in. The mansion, the housekeepers, and the afternoon teas were not coming with me.

There had been reminders through the years that I shouldn't get too comfortable. My student loans, grants, and financial aid hadn't been enough to cover all of my bills, so throughout college, I was always working some odd job. First came the work-study job at the student gym on campus. Then the job walking people to their tables at Miyagi's on Sunset, a sushi bar turned nightclub in the evenings, often frequented by Fabio, Pamela Anderson, and 'N Sync. Next were a few random acting and modeling jobs. And during my senior year, I became a hostess at a high-end French restaurant in Downtown LA. It was the kind of place that served rabbit and had a sommelier on call to help pick out the perfect burgundy on the way to the symphony.

Each night after my shift, I was given the perk of ordering one thing off the dinner menu. I used the time to continue Abi's etiquette lessons and expand my knowledge of food, wine, and music—trying quail and duck for the first time, falling in love with bossa nova, and learning how to pronounce *foie gras* and *mille-feuille*. Why was I so preoccupied with manners, pronouncing food names correctly, and learning wine basics at twenty-one? I felt like I needed to be constantly in preparation mode. If I stopped, I might be caught off guard and risk humiliating myself. The life I'd lived for the previous four years—the house, the housekeepers, the parties, the friends, the opportunities—had seemed to appear out of thin air, and it felt like it could disappear just as quickly.

By spring of senior year, the Chutes and Social Ladders seemed scattered around me like booby traps. I'd received no job offers from my unpaid summer internships, and I hadn't been called in for any interviews for the journalist positions I'd applied for. I didn't have parents who could support me financially or who had social networks that could help me land a job at a newspaper. And I was leaving school with over $50,000 in student loan debt.

I was disappointed in myself when I realized that I'd have to wait tables after graduation until I could figure something else out. But I had no other option. And to top it all off, my mom had invited my father to graduation *again*.

To keep things interesting, this time he was coming with a younger sister of mine that I didn't know existed.

I had made it so far—farther than I'd expected I would—and I had technically done everything right. The academic foundation for my career as a journalist had been set and I was graduating cum laude with departmental honors from Annenberg, yet the rug still felt like it could be pulled out from under me at any moment.

The day before graduation, I packed my clothes in cardboard boxes and walked down the grand staircase of the Tri Delt house to our elegant foyer for the last time. Looking around the silent mansion and thinking back on the anxiety-ridden girl who first walked through those doors in her wannabe-chola war paint, I couldn't help but wonder, had it all been enough? I had contorted and polished myself like a brand-new penny during my time at USC, but I was still graduating with no job and no safety net. Would I be able to hustle my way into a well-paying career? Or would the sorority house end up being the nicest place I ever lived?

CHAPTER SIX

ON THE BOUND

Y ou should just move back into your old bedroom," my mom urged weeks before graduation, when I told her I hadn't been able to find a job. "Your sister can sleep with me in my room."

I was visiting home to play with Monica, now an eight-year-old gymnast with ringlet curls who followed me around like a shadow. She looked up at me from her cereal bowl with big, hopeful eyes, but I quickly shut it down.

"I don't think that's the best idea," I started.

"Well, then you better take the first job you can find. It's really hard to get a job right now, you know. What are you going to do for money in the meantime? Do you have money for a security deposit? And have you thought about health insurance?" She had stopped chopping vegetables for Abi's chicken-soup recipe and was looking at me, waiting for answers.

I could feel my body clench as I reacted to her fear, doubts entering my mind. I didn't have answers to any of her questions. She was coming from a place of protectiveness, but it felt like she was asking me to look down at the ground while I was scaling a cliff.

When you chase dreams that your family doesn't understand, your choices can often be questioned repeatedly—at the very moments when hesitation and skepticism can be the most damaging. How could I explain to her that moving home felt like moving backward—geographically and emotionally. There was no *way* I was doing it.

For First and Onlys, the people who love us the most don't always get the difference between finding a job and trying to build a career. They see ambition as good, but the unpredictable maneuvering that comes along with it? Not so much. Often, our seemingly reckless choices don't make sense to them. Working unpaid internships, taking crappy interim positions, switching from job to job—why would we do these things and how are they even helping? Wasn't getting and *staying* in a good job the whole point of going to college?

My relatives scratched their heads that I took on debt to go to USC and then didn't snatch up the first reliable position I could find. The messages I received from my mom and from other family members were simple: Land a decent paycheck immediately, and hold on to it as long as you can. Oh, and live at home or as close to home as possible.

But I wanted something different.

Given their past experiences with sudden layoffs and unemployment—as well as the common practice of multigenerational living in Latino culture—their perspectives were understandable. Still, I couldn't be around that kind of thinking if I was going to take the kinds of risks—and make the sacrifices—required to pursue a career in journalism. There's a saying: Don't ask people who have never been where you are going for directions. So I asked no one for their opinion, figured out the least amount of money I could survive on each month, made a plan to share an apartment with three friends from USC, and got to work.

During my first year out of college, I waited on hundreds of tables and reported on zero stories. I told myself to be patient, that these things take time, but I was desperately searching for a break. When a friend of mine mentioned that he knew someone in news who might be hiring, I begged him to help me get an interview.

Weeks later, I was sitting across from a hotshot news director in his thirties, in what I considered to be the most pivotal job interview of my nonexistent career as a journalist. It was also the *only* job interview of my career as a journalist up until that point. Every other résumé I'd previously sent had been kindly declined without so much as meeting me in person. Landing this interview was the most progress I'd made, and I convinced myself that this had been my intended path all along.

"If I were to hire you, what would you want to report on?" the news director asked, tapping his pen on the desk. He was clean-cut and wearing a wrinkleless blue dress shirt with cuff links. I'd noticed him looking me up and down when I walked into his glass-walled office moments earlier.

He had the authority to hire talent, but judging by the way he leaned back in his chair, he was going to make me work for it. I was ready. In preparation for our meeting, I had pored over news stories and had ideas and pitches jotted down in my notebook.

"I'm interested in covering access to healthcare, the housing crisis, and immigration reform. I want to explore the kinds of stories that usually aren't told—"

"Yeah, yeah, I got it," he said, cutting me off. "But what about other types of stories? Not what's obviously already on local news here in LA."

He chuckled, one of his shiny black dress shoes tapping on the carpet. Each time he checked his watch, it was becoming clearer that he saw our meeting as more of a favor for a friend than a real interview.

"Tell me…which countries have you traveled to? Because our correspondents travel all around the world reporting on investigative stories. They're in the field *all* the time. Cambodia, Vietnam, the Middle East, South Africa. Where would you want to travel to, and to cover what specifically? It's a pretty big world out there, you know."

My cheeks began to get hot as he launched into the credentials of the other reporters on his staff—their alma maters, the newspapers they read daily, the places they'd been, the groundbreaking investigations they'd worked on, and most pointedly, their insatiable curiosity. It felt like he was daring me to prove that I was one of them—a.k.a. the worldly, smart people.

I stared down at my hands to think, as the seconds of silence grew excruciating. I wanted to be the person he was describing. More than anything. But there was a reason I hadn't even considered getting on a plane for ten years and still couldn't now, and it was bigger than the fact that I didn't have the money for a ticket.

"Take a minute," he said, getting up. "I'll be right back."

As I watched the news director walk out of the office, it felt like my chances of being hired went out the door with him. I was embarrassed. He'd obviously been able to tell that I was struggling. I tried to concentrate on coming up with international story ideas, but my mind kept going back to Paris.

When I was around nine years old, my mom briefly worked as a secretary at the now-defunct Mexicana Airlines, a thankless job that came with one huge perk: flying standby on the airline for free. It was the only way we could afford to travel back then, and we mostly took short flights with my aunts to Mexico—Cancún, Puerto Vallarta, and Mexico City. In photos of that era, my mom and my aunts are mostly in bathing suits on sun-drenched beaches, while I pose, gap-toothed, at their side.

Yet before we made it down my mom's list of Mexican resort towns, she was let go in a wave of massive layoffs. On top of losing a decent-paying job with benefits, she would also be giving up her treasured ability to fly for free. My mom knew that without her employee discount, she'd probably never be able to afford traveling to Europe, and there was one place she just had to see. This was likely her best, and last, chance to ever go to Paris.

My mom may not have been exposed to many

international cities, but she'd seen postcards on the Venice Beach Boardwalk of the majestic Eiffel Tower at sunset and imagined herself strolling down cobblestone streets. For her last freebie trip, she booked the two of us on a flight to Paris for nine days, with stops in Belgium and Germany. I loved everything about traveling back then—the frantic bustle of the airport and even the musty smell of the airplane. I could hardly sit still in my seat as we waited to board at LAX.

The trip started off as expected. We ate flaky baguettes on the grass in the Champ de Mars and saw red-lipped women dance the cancan, wearing bejeweled bikini tops and crimson feathers on their heads, at the Moulin Rouge. But when the streets emptied and it was time to sleep in our matching twin-sized beds, my mom tossed and turned until the sun came up. She had never experienced such a dramatic change in time zones—having only been in Mexico and California—and she didn't know how to handle her extreme jet lag.

With each sleepless night, her exhaustion turned more and more into panic. As a child in Mexico, my mom had often forced herself to stay awake at night, in an effort to keep Abi company whenever my grandfather came home drunk. That habit later morphed into bouts of insomnia, set off whenever she felt alone or unprotected. Unbeknownst to my mom when we were in Paris, the jet lag she was experiencing was triggering all of her childhood PTSD. I'd wake up throughout night to the sound of crying, and lie there staring at the ceiling with a knot in my stomach, not understanding what was wrong or how to help.

By day four, my mom's eyes were red and bleary, her skin was pale, and her body was weak from sleep deprivation. She told me to pack my suitcase, and we rushed to the airport with the intention of getting on any standby flight that would have us. As I ran behind my mom through the international terminal, dragging my suitcase behind me, she collapsed onto the floor. Strangers and various airport personnel descended upon us, speaking only French. My mom lay there unresponsive.

Suddenly, all of the ways I was able to help at home as a mini-adult were unavailable to me. I couldn't understand what anyone was saying. I slowly moved off to the side, terror-stricken, as more and more people crowded around her. I saw someone bend down and pick up her wrist to feel her pulse, and was certain my mom was about to die. And then what would happen to me? I would be left abandoned in a foreign country with no way to communicate, no place to stay, no money for food, no plane ticket home, and no grown-up to take care of me. And then I would either die too or be stolen away by bad people. I was sure of it.

When the medics arrived and my mom finally started to stir, I felt reassured, but not entirely, because our circumstances were unchanged. We were still trapped in Paris.

My mom rented us a cheap room at a hotel by the airport and called home to my grandparents to beg them to send money for plane tickets. As I sat on the bed in our hotel room, I heard her say to them that we had to leave immediately or she wasn't "going to make it." I didn't cry. I didn't ask any questions. I didn't say I was hungry. I just sat still, with my hands in my lap, and prayed that someone would save us before my mom died for real this time. Thankfully, my aunt Nannette had recently gotten her first credit card, and the next day we were able to leave Paris on what felt like a never-ending succession of layover flights until we finally made it home to LA.

In the aftermath, my mom lost her nerve to travel, and two years later I'd have that massive panic attack on the plane to visit my father. So, no, I hadn't traveled much, and my "curiosity" to see the world had been a bit stifled. I knew my fear was irrational, but my panic attacks didn't.

I certainly didn't feel that explaining any of this to the news director would help my case. From his tone, it seemed like he'd already concluded that the lack of travel in my recent past showed me to be an incurious person anyway. Someone who didn't have all that much depth.

When he returned to the office, I tried my best to pitch some international story ideas on the spot, but his mind was already made up. I walked back to my car after a polite handshake and realized that the career trajectory I'd been aiming for was probably not going to materialize. At least not anytime soon. I could keep submitting my résumé to the same handful of networks in LA, but I might as well have been dropping it into a black hole somewhere. It felt like I was back to square one, all of the progress I'd made at USC gone.

I'd thought that earning a college degree meant I was relatively set. That was how it had been sold to me, and that was certainly what my family thought. College was supposed to be an instantaneous economic-mobility generator. I also grew up around the idea that our families sacrifice to give us better lives—a common refrain for children of immigrants—and that a college degree is exhibit A of that better life. But as many First and Onlys discover, a diploma is just the beginning. A degree alone won't propel us into homeownership or a good retirement. It's the first summit we scale, only to realize from the top that there's a larger, steeper mountain still ahead. And that mountain rarely comes with a built-in expert guide, in other words, a family member or friend who has connections in the industry or who can give us firsthand advice.

Until I could figure out another way to break into journalism, I'd have to be resourceful, which meant I'd need to take every opportunity to make money and, if I was lucky, to start making a name for myself. And so began the hardest period of striving in my life: the Lonely Hustle.

Hustling certainly isn't unique to First and Onlys, but in our case, the drive behind it is magnified. It's one thing to hustle because you have big goals and aspirations, and it's quite another when your ambitions are overlaid with the understanding that there really is no other option. You *must* figure this out, or risk compromising not only your future but that of your family. It's not only your own survival in the balance; it's also the welfare of the people you love.

I was very much on my own at this stage of my life. I knew I couldn't move home—even if it would have been the best way to save money—because in part, my success was contingent on being *away* from the nervous energy of my family. Many First and Onlys have enmeshed family systems, and oftentimes, claiming our independence means having to break those established family bonds. It's messy and sometimes taken the wrong way. And that's why I call it the Lonely Hustle. When First and Onlys hit the streets, they usually have to do it alone.

Working a side hustle was already second nature to me. I'd had a job ever since high school, when I was hired to stand on a platform as a live mannequin on the Venice Boardwalk, while '90s Enigma blasted out of speakers overhead. I knew how to get creative.

Over the next three years post college, I was a club promoter for a Mexican cantina and a dancer in music videos for Justin Timberlake and Smash Mouth. After showing up to "open call day" for a modeling agency, I walked out with an agent and a job as a calendar girl (as Miss November, I dressed as an astronaut and hung from the ceiling in a harness). I appeared in the film *The Aviator* with Leonardo DiCaprio, shot a beer commercial with Ben Stiller, was a member of a pop-singing girl group, walked in a fashion show for Skechers, was featured on gel bottles for Paul Mitchell hair products, and waited tables at a candlelit steak house in Venice.

I was all over the place, but I was working regularly and buying myself time while I figured out my next move. And then I got a call from my modeling agent that was considered to be a big "get." *Maxim* was interested in interviewing me.

My agent insisted that it was a no-brainer, and that by simply appearing in the magazine I'd book a *lot* more work. Plus, I would be exclusively featured as "one to watch" and a "rising star."

"They're giving you a full-page interview *and* a photo shoot with one of their top photographers!" she stressed.

Sensing my hesitation, she added, "You're not going to be the table of contents girl. It'll be an actual article about *you*. Who you are. Trust me—they don't do this for just anyone."

Telling myself that I was not in a position to be turning down a profile piece that could lead to an opportunity, I agreed to the interview.

Weeks later, I sat in my living room at 6 a.m., wearing sweats and no makeup, waiting for a car to arrive and take me to some undisclosed location for the shoot. I had a bit of what-did-I-get-myself-into butterflies, but I talked them down, reminding myself about the one-on-one I had scheduled with one of *Maxim*'s reporters the following week. Through my window, I saw an elegant black stretch limo slowly pull up to the curb. *See?* I told myself, feeling reassured. *There's nothing to be stressed out about.*

As I was driven up a winding road into the Hollywood Hills, I sipped on the chilled bottled water that had been placed next to my seat and imagined the stylish designer clothes I was about to be wearing. The whole thing felt glamorous—the driver, the palm trees, the location in the Hills. We pulled up to a white, modern estate at the very top, as dozens of crew members milled about preparing for the shoot.

Turning three with my mom and Abi

My great-grandparents Alfonso and Maria Elena in Sonora, Mexico, in the early 1920s

My grandparents Bernardo (Abito) and Maria Louisa (Abi)...the way they looked at each other!

Abi and Abito soon after they were married

Abi holding Aunt Nannette, with my mom (left) and Aunt Elizabeth (right)

Aunt Nannette (left) and my mom (right) with Abito, newly arrived in LA from Tecate, Mexico, in the 1970s

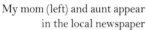

My mom (left) and aunt appear in the local newspaper

My mom (left) and aunt as extras in the 1970s Chicano gang movie *Walk Proud*

The only picture I have of my parents together

Baby me with the four Medellin sisters, my uncles, and Abi

Birthday piñata at Marine Park

Mall photo with my mom

Playing with Abito in our living room

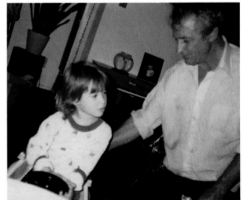

The play closet!

Our apartment on Marine, in the bedroom my aunts shared where we prayed our novenas (not sure who the baby is)

Waiting for the Big
Blue Bus #3

Sitting on our balcony after
Abi pin-curled my hair

Abi and me in Hawaii, courtesy
of my mom's free standby tickets
from Mexicana Airlines

The headshot for
Mac and Me and
Purple People Eater

In a photo booth with Abi, baby Monica, and my mom (post-Mario)

Rehearsing a play for the Virginia Avenue Project with Leigh

Virginia Park days
and the black pager
from Costco

Little Monica (and
big hair)

The last picture I have
with Abi before she
passed away

The one-AM-station Mercury Capri and the Delta Delta Delta sorority house in the background

With a sorority sister during sophomore year

The "smallest diamond you've ever seen"

Mother-daughter tea at the Ritz

A shoot in the early '00s

My blink-and-you-miss-it appearance as a red-eyed demon hunted by Keanu Reeves in *Constantine* Credit: *Still from Constantine, Warner Brothers Pictures, 2005*

Waiting tables at Gladstones and yes, that's clam chowder on my jeans

Tailgating with friends during our first year at Harvard

Bringing Selena and mariachis to the Kennedy School talent show

With friends (and the inflatable globe) at Harvard Commencement, '08

Outside the West Wing lobby with my mom and Monica

A pinch-me moment about to board Air Force One

Briefing President Obama in the Oval Office before his *Latina Magazine* interview
Credit: Pete Souza, Chief Official White House Photographer

Last day at the White House

Canvassing for my congressional campaign with volunteers and supporters

With students at a Cal State LA event

Speaking at a candidate forum

A candid moment looking at Abi's photo with my mom, while filming my campaign ad

Christmas morning with the fireplace Abi made out of cardboard and foil

"Talent is here," I heard someone announce as I was led through the sleek interior and into the makeup and wardrobe room. It made me feel important.

And then I saw them:

Two racks of hangers holding the strips of tiny fabric that were to be my wardrobe.

It may sound naive that I was surprised by this, given that it was *Maxim* and all, but I had assumed that being a featured up-and-comer with my own article meant that I'd be treated more like one of the known actresses or pop singers I'd seen featured in the magazine. They were dressed sexy but more covered up. I'd also assumed that my agent had negotiated my wardrobe beforehand and that there would at least be a range of options for me to choose from.

"Try these on, sweetheart," the stylist said, handing me what appeared to be a couple of see-through pieces of ribbon. I felt horrified. I was nowhere near confident enough with my body to wear something like that, and it wasn't the way I'd expected to be represented. I wanted to run back to the limo as fast as I could, but at the same time, I didn't feel like I had any power to leave or to object. Besides, I was used to saying yes when I wanted to say no. So I obediently went into the bathroom and tried to strategically place the fabric to drape over as much of my chest as possible.

I must've looked as uncomfortable as I felt when I emerged, because the stylist took one look at me and said, "Let's try something else, sweetie."

We settled on the most "conservative" option—a black lace contraption that covered up more of my torso than a bikini, along with black lace heels. Over the next couple of hours, I posed next to a red velvet curtain and against a plain white wall while a team of editorial staff watched closely and the photographer called out directions. *Push out your hips! Sexy to the camera! Arch your back! Arch more! More!* It was the most unsexy I'd ever felt.

When I got home later that night, I was more worried than excited about what kind of image would be chosen to appear in the glossy pages. Did it even matter anymore what I'd say in my interview the following week? I had considered modeling to be a temporary job on my road to becoming a journalist, and hadn't previously given much thought to whether or not it might actually negatively impact my future career. But taking these photos had felt like a step too far. Would they ever come back to haunt me?

After that, I did get more job offers, only not the kind I wanted. When my *Maxim* issue hit the stands and casting agents saw my spread, I heard from Adam Carolla's *The Man Show*, to see if I would jump on a trampoline in skimpy lingerie on air, Charlie Sheen's *Two and a Half Men*, to see if I would guest-star on the sitcom while wearing a string bikini, and pretty much every trashy show on television. I turned them all down.

Far from feeling complimented, I found all the new attention to be upsetting. Judging from the offers I was receiving, the photos had seemed to send a message that I was a willing participant in the commodification of female sexuality. The same objectification through the male gaze that I had dissected in my gender studies classes as USC.

And I hated that. I also resented that it felt like I'd now checked the "sexy box" in my what-kind-of-woman-are-you survey, eliminating all other options in the eyes of society. Particularly the "smart box." Because God forbid a woman be both. It all brought to mind a run-in I'd had with Mike Wallace when I was just a kid.

I couldn't have been more than ten years old when we crossed paths, and I was deep in my awkward preteen phase. It was the late '80s, when I had string beans for legs and wore multiple neon scrunchies sloppily wrapped around my side ponytail. Mike Wallace, legendary journalist on CBS's *60 Minutes*, was the star presenter at a career-day event for school-age children in LA, and I centered my schedule around attending his lecture on how to be a great interviewer.

His talk took place in a giant hall with rows upon rows of folding chairs, but every single seat was taken. I sat in the back, scribbling notes in my wide-ringed notebook and plotting how I'd steal a moment to ask him a few questions. When the lecture was over, half the audience surged to the front of the room, yet I hung back. My strategy was to let everyone go ahead of me so that by being last, our conversation wouldn't be rushed or interrupted. Twenty minutes later, the room had cleared, and I had my chance.

I approached him with as much confidence as I could muster.

"Nice to meet you, Mr. Wallace. I want to have a career like yours. Do you have any advice for me?"

I had my notebook out and ready.

"My advice to you is this," he said dryly, underscoring each word.

He looked me right in the eyes.

"Don't expect to get anywhere in your career just because you're pretty."

Considering that I slept in dorky headgear to fix the gap in between my two front teeth and still played with Barbies, that was the last thing I expected to come out of his mouth. It felt like he was accusing me of doing something wrong, but I didn't understand what exactly. Red-faced, I quickly thanked him and got out of there. But his words stayed with me.

As I grew older, I became increasingly self-conscious about what kind of young woman I was perceived to be. I wanted to be seen as respectable and intelligent, yet sexualized gender stereotypes seemed hidden around every corner, like land mines waiting to go off. In one of my gender studies courses at USC, I tried to unpack feminine archetypes and even wrote a research paper challenging the notion of "sluts vs. prudes." Yet now, after the *Maxim* article, I felt as though I had become a case study myself.

By all accounts, I had hustled my way into a potentially lucrative career in entertainment, but I felt objectified and miserable. I was paying $500 a month to sleep on a lumpy futon in my friend's barren living room, dodging sleazy job offers, and waiting tables at a tourist-trap seafood restaurant on the Pacific Coast Highway.

Gladstones in Malibu had everything an out-of-towner came to the West Coast to experience—rolling blue Pacific waves, fresh seafood towers overflowing with oysters and lobster, and a daily sing-along of Randy Newman's "I Love L.A." at sunset. A friend who worked there had encouraged me to apply, bragging that the checks (and therefore the tips) were big. I could think of worse things than waiting tables in the ocean breeze, feet from the sand. Before long, I was wearing a white cotton T-shirt with dancing crabs on it, wrapping people's leftovers in gold aluminum foil in the shape of a whale, and serving mounds of fried shrimp to tourists, Jessica Simpson, and even Suge Knight.

In that setting—clam-chowder-stained shirt, standing on a table singing "I Love L.A." every day—it was impossible not to face the fact that I wasn't just putting in time as an LA hyphenate (actress-model) while making progress toward a career as a reporter. I was a waiter. Period. And while there was certainly nothing wrong with being a waiter, I had believed it when I'd told myself at graduation that this was all nothing more than a necessary, and temporary, stepping stone.

But as one year turned into three, I couldn't see a path out of the restaurant kitchen anymore. I found myself counting crumpled dollar bills at the end of my shift with the same hand-to-mouth energy I had seen in my family and had worked so hard to avoid.

And just when it seemed like things couldn't get any more discouraging, my mom called me from the Kaiser Permanente medical center in West LA, choking on her breath. She was bawling and I could barely understand what she was saying, but I made out the word *cancer*, and dread began to reverberate throughout my body. Unbeknownst to me, she had felt a small lump in one of her breasts and had been going in for tests and inconclusive biopsies for months before finally being diagnosed. I was her very first call.

I jumped right into parent mode, trying to calm and comfort her while suppressing my own tears. Still, all I could think was, *This is it. She's going to die....Just like Abi did.*

I could tell my mom was thinking the same thing, and who could really blame either of us? After how traumatizing it had been to lose my grandmother mere months after her breast cancer diagnosis, we both now shared Abi's belief that a cancer diagnosis was as good as a death sentence. One day Abi was making us her tamales with the surprise pimento olive at the center, and the next we were burying her on a grassy hill overlooking the city. I still hadn't recovered from losing her so quickly.

When I was a child, keeping my mom safe and happy was my primary focus. Back then, my survival depended on it, but even now, as an adult, her well-being felt entangled with my own. It was excruciating to be powerless over the final outcome, so I spent hours researching her cancer and her treatment options online. With Abi gone and my father who knows where, my mom was all I had.

And what about my eleven-year-old sister, whose own father rarely came around? What would happen to her if our mom died? Monica was a tenderhearted kid back then, obsessed with SpongeBob and playing soccer on a team called the Purple Princesses. This would absolutely destroy her.

I knew what I'd do: quit trying to follow my passions,

get a random office job, and raise my sister. Was I ready to be a mom at twenty-four years old with negative dollars to my name? No. Was I ready to lose my mom? No way. And yet my life felt like it was careening toward that very path.

The only hope I held on to was chemo. It hadn't worked for my grandmother, but maybe since my mom's cancer had been caught earlier, she still had a chance. I insisted on coming along to all of her doctor's appointments to make sure that we came up with the very best treatment plan possible. We had to do whatever it took to beat this thing.

Days later, we sat together in a white shoebox of a room, waiting for her oncologist—my mom in a baby-blue hospital gown, and me sitting on a cold plastic chair at her feet.

"I don't think I can do chemo," my mom said resolutely to the HMO doctor, as he strolled in over an hour late to her appointment. I'd read every flyer on the dingy wall while we waited, anticipating that we wouldn't be given much time.

"What do you mean?" I practically shouted, not believing what I'd heard.

They both looked at me, startled, and then back at each other.

"Cecilia, I have to advise you to do chemo," the oncologist said. "Your breast cancer is triple-negative. It is a much more aggressive type of cancer that has a significantly higher rate of recurrence." Even he seemed shocked.

My mom's eyes swelled with tears. "I'll get depressed again, Doctor. I can't handle it. I know myself, and...I just can't do chemo!" She was wailing loudly now, and I started shaking my leg absentmindedly.

When we reached the hospital parking lot after her appointment, I turned to my mom and looked her in the eyes.

"I want you to hear every word of what I'm about to say," I whispered with hushed outrage as patients walked past us on their way to the ER. "If you don't do chemo, I will never speak to you again." My hands were shaking as I fumbled through my purse for the car keys.

Hot tears streamed down her cheeks. "I'm sorry I'm weak. But I can't do it. Please forgive me."

"I'm serious. I will *never* speak to you again," I said, nausea gripping my throat.

I dropped her off at home and pulled over to cry in my car. The last thing I wanted to do was threaten my mom. I knew she was terrified. But I also couldn't let her give up, leaving my sister and me essentially parentless.

A week passed of no contact. It was brutal to not check in with my mom. Yet I didn't budge, even when she sent me a long, handwritten letter explaining why she wouldn't be doing chemo and apologizing for letting me down. I'd pick up my sister and take her out for ice cream, but I wouldn't set foot in my mom's apartment.

Another week or so passed, and then she called.

"Okay," she whimpered.

"Okay what?" I asked, holding my breath.

"I'll do it," she said, and we sniffled over the phone at each other, both in tears. "I'm only doing it because of you…I can't not talk to you. I love you so much."

The betrayal I had been feeling instantly lifted. She *would* fight after all—for herself and for us. It was the most motherly thing she had ever done.

"I love you too," I told her, "and I promise I'll help."

Not long after, I moved back into my mom's apartment. Monica was now in my old bedroom, so I bought an air mattress and camped out on the floor of the tiny living room.

For the next five months, I spent my days serving steaming bowl after bowl of clam chowder, and my nights waking up with my mom when she went to the bathroom to throw up during chemo. I was exhausted, and my hair permanently smelled like fish. I may have been greeting my tables with a big smile, but inside, I was inundated with what-ifs and playing Fiona Apple songs on repeat.

Watching my mom endure agony—knowing that it was *my* fault for pushing her into it—filled me with guilt. Would the chemo even end up working? *Was* it making her depressed again?

Then my attention would turn to Monica. How would I shield her from the worst of it, or pull off being a single mom on a waiter's salary?

And finally, there was the question that felt selfish to even consider but that haunted me all the same: Was I prepared to give up on all of my own dreams?

One afternoon, I was alone in the restaurant kitchen, preparing a tray of lemon-and-kale garnishes. I could feel dampness soaking my shirt from leaning up against the fish-juice-drenched counter, and my fingers were burning from the acidity of the lemon wedges I was slicing. There was a window that separated the kitchen from the outdoor patio, so that diners could watch the cooks prepare their food. Out of the corner of my eye, I could see a few people ogling me like I was a sideshow, as I lined up my garnishes in neat rows on the tray. *Get me out of here*, I thought.

Maybe it was the experience of being stared at by strangers during one of my lowest points, or maybe I'd reached the limit of feeling utterly disappointed in myself and paralyzed about the future, but I began to feel the kitchen walls closing in on me. The familiar warning signs of an approaching panic attack came on: rapid heartbeat, body tingling, hands shaking.

I had two choices at that moment: sink into a pool of hopelessness or kick *hard* against the bottom and try to reach for the surface. As I finished my fourth tray of garnishes—lemon, then kale, then lemon, then kale—I gathered every last shred of nerve I had left and steadied my breath. A feeling of certainty overcame me, and I knew what to do: I'd apply to graduate school.

I won't pretend that I had this grand epiphany and then forged ahead on a clear new pathway, like they do in the movies. My time in the Lonely Hustle was just getting started. I was twenty-four with nothing to show for it but a brief appearance as a demon hunted by Keanu Reeves in the movie *Constantine* and a deep knowledge of wild Alaskan king salmon. I was getting nowhere fast.

My previous plan of becoming a journalist seemed to require a certain degree of luck, and I didn't have the luxury of waiting around anymore. In my mind, I needed a sure thing so I'd be prepared to raise my sister without inadvertently creating my nightmare scenario—a life spent stressed about money.

A graduate degree was as close as I could get to a real guarantee that I'd be able to support myself (and Monica, if need be) in the future. Growing up, I had heard my family refer to those with higher degrees as an elite group. It was similar to how they had talked about getting a college degree, but way more impressive and exclusive. People with master's degrees were "white-collar," my mom had said. If the only thing separating me from them was another piece of paper, then I'd switch gears and go get that one too.

Deciding what type of graduate school I'd attend had an eeny-meeny-miny-moe quality to it. I had no personal network of people with advanced degrees to offer advice. In 2003, when I was exploring my options, less than 2 percent of Latinas in the US held a graduate degree. My choice pretty much came down to a process of elimination. I knew I didn't want to be a doctor or a lawyer, so I crossed out med school and law school right off the bat. Then a friend from college who was taking a GMAT prep course for business school offered to bring me to a class as a guest so I could check it out. Business school seemed broad enough. Maybe that was the best way to cover all my bases.

The GMAT instructor was a bespectacled cycling enthusiast named Robert. He was skinny, with a crew cut, sprinkled the math version of dad jokes into his lectures, and loved the GMAT as if it were the Dodgers. Students lined up each semester to get into his standing-room-only course that all but guaranteed to raise your scores. On my first day, Robert handed me a practice test to get an idea of my baseline. I had always assumed that since I'd done well in high school math and didn't have to take it in college, I was all set. But as I stared at problem sets with no clue where to even begin, I realized that not all high school math educations are created equal.

"Didn't you take algebra in high school? Geometry?" Robert asked, after scoring my test.

"Yes, but it was nothing like this. I've never seen these types of math problems."

"Wow, this is not good," he said, shaking his head. "You can't get into any good business school with this math score. Definitely not top thirty. You're going to need to raise it by at least two hundred points, which is a *lot*."

I was sure that taking Robert's class would improve my math score, but each of his three-month courses cost more than $650. I was living off $1,200 a month. Then my mom's words—*You don't ask, you don't get*—rang in my ears. There was only a month left in the current course, so I asked Robert if I might be able to sit in for the rest of it.

"I'll squat in the back. You won't even know I'm there," I promised.

"Ahhh, I usually don't do that. But okay, fine," he said, relenting. "We'll see where your scores are next month and then go from there."

I went on to take Robert's course four consecutive times. Since each one was over three months and sixty hours long, that's over 240 hours of formal GMAT prep. While my friends were going out to beach bars, I was sitting at the kitchen table trying to grasp math concepts I should've learned when I was sixteen. It was demoralizing to see that each obstacle I faced in the past only compounded the size of the obstacle I was facing in the future—a snowball effect of social barriers. No matter how many practice tests I took, my score wouldn't budge for months.

Once again, my family had no frame of reference for how hard I was working, so I rarely shared what I was up to. I purposely kept everything to myself for fear that their lukewarm reactions would dissuade me from even trying. One day, at lunch with my mom and her friend, I made the mistake of letting my guard down and confessing that I was trying to apply to grad school.

"Are you kidding? That's a waste of money and time," my mom's friend Jade said emphatically. "Why don't you get something reliable and secure, like a job as an assistant to a big executive, like what I'm doing?" Her wrists and neck were adorned with garish gold jewelry, courtesy of the married man she was dating.

My mom nodded in agreement. "Maybe you should listen to what she has to say," she chimed in. "Jade has experience in the corporate world."

I was working harder than I ever had, but I couldn't prove to them that I was making the right choices. Yet that's exactly what many First and Onlys are often asked to do, the subtext of which is "don't rise above your station." It felt unfair to be questioned and discouraged from pursuing the same goal that I imagined many of my GMAT classmates were being applauded for.

"This is ultimately going to lead to something better," I said.

Jade looked at me like I was naive.

Maybe I was. I had no way of knowing that my GMAT prep was going to pay off. I had no guarantee that I could raise my math score. If I did raise my math score, I had no guarantee that I would get into a decent graduate school. And even if I managed that, I had no guarantee that a master's degree would launch my career. All I had was my gut and a commitment to see things through.

During the two years I took (and retook and retook and retook) Robert's course, I hustled every which way I could think of to make myself an attractive candidate to graduate schools. As my math score started to creep up, I wanted to feel optimistic, but it was still nowhere near as high as it needed to be.

Sensing my discouragement, Robert shifted my focus to the other elements of a solid MBA application that I still had to ace: great extracurriculars and an impressive job. First, I signed up for several professional fellowships, sporting Forever 21 blazers to full-day workshops on Saturdays at UCLA, as a part of a pre-MBA program for applicants of color.

Then, I applied for a junior-level grantmaking job at a statewide health foundation, on a team that focused on agricultural workers. When I read the job description—funding wellness programs for farmworkers, many of whom were undocumented—I was convinced that this was finally an opportunity to merge my day job with my passion, something I had been struggling to find ever since college. And when I was flatly rejected, for having no relevant experience (commercials and clam chowder didn't count), I started volunteering at a nonprofit my interviewer had name-dropped during our meeting. First and Onlys are rarely deterred by the first rejection, after all. "No" is assumed, and simply means it's time to recalibrate and find another way.

Months later, I reapplied to the foundation with my new nonprofit volunteer experience at the top of my résumé, and got the job the second time around. I joyfully gave notice at Gladstones, moving off the air mattress at my mom's apartment and into my own place, where I slept in an actual bedroom. I threw away all those smelly T-shirts and scoured sale racks for cardigans and work dresses. I bought a desk mug with a large cursive A on it and tacked up photos of my friends and family on the walls of my very own cubicle.

When it was time to officially take the GMAT at a test center, I completed the exam yet hesitated before clicking the button to preview my final score. This was it. The moment when I'd learn if the past two years had been a total waste of time or the pivot point I'd been hoping for. I said a quick prayer and clicked. I'd raised my score exactly 220 points, putting me within striking range for a top MBA program.

Smiling at the screen, I gathered my things in a hurry so I could run out to the parking lot and call Robert. It felt as if I'd been given a second chance across the board. Modeling was behind me. Waiting tables was behind me. My mom had finished chemo and had recently been declared cancer-free. She and my little sister would be okay, and I was free to start an MBA program the next fall. All that was left were the applications.

"Aren't you applying to an Ivy League?" Robert said while looking over my list of target schools. We were sitting in my kitchen on a Saturday afternoon, final drafts of my essays in neat stacks on the table in front of me. Robert had offered to read over my personal statements one last time before I submitted my applications.

Applying to an Ivy League school hadn't even occurred to me. In my mind, they were for senators' kids or people who had *III* after their name. There's a cluster of streets named after Ivy League schools in Santa Monica—Yale, Princeton, and Harvard. Sometimes, while in the area, I'd purposely drive down one of those streets for fun. That was the closest I thought I'd ever get to an Ivy League.

"No, I didn't plan to," I responded. Was he really suggesting—

"Come on, you're aiming too low!" he said, shaking his head.

I wasn't used to anyone encouraging me to be more bold than I already was, and I realized how much I craved being egged on versus discouraged. How alone and underestimated I'd felt up until then.

"If you were to pick just one," he said, "which would it be?"

Harvard, I thought. In my twenty-six-year-old eyes, it was the brass ring.

"You know Harvard has the Kennedy School too," he said, reading my mind. "The Kennedy School of Government? You should apply there as well."

I had never heard of a school of government before. I grabbed my laptop and googled the Kennedy School, clicking on the page for the Master in Public Policy (MPP) program. The words *Make a difference in the world* jumped out at me in bold lettering.

Make a difference. That was what I'd been wanting to do ever since my days sweeping leaves with Abi. I just didn't know how one went about it. There was an entire school dedicated to finding ways to make a difference?

"This is amazing. Hand me my list," I said to Robert, who smiled as he passed me the sheet of paper.

At the bottom of a long lineup of business schools, I wrote, "Harvard Kennedy School." It was a Hail Mary pass— and the program I was suddenly the most excited about.

If I wanted to make a difference, it was hard to think of something more fitting than studying public policy. But was I really Ivy League material? Visions in my head of privileged, preppy geniuses in striped scarves all pointed to no.

A few months later, I was sitting in my cubicle at the foundation when an email from Harvard admissions appeared in my inbox. I held my breath as I logged on to my account and read the first line: *Welcome to the Harvard Kennedy School of Government's Class of 2008!*

As I read the rest of the letter, I slowly stood up at my desk, feeling the impulse to scream or jump or run down the hall telling every person who would listen. Instead, I just stood there and absorbed the enormity of the moment.

After a long grind, everything was about to change drastically again. Another social ladder had appeared in front of me, and this one was taller and more dazzling than any of the previous ones. Just a couple of years after appearing in *Maxim* and slinging clam chowder in Malibu, I had the golden ticket—an acceptance letter to Harvard.

CHAPTER SEVEN

HOW TO SAVE A LIFE

THE FIRST FEW weeks after I received my acceptance letter, I lost myself in daydreams of strolling to class through Harvard Square under fiery autumn leaves, hands in the pockets of a beige trench coat. I'd get to be Ali McGraw in *Love Story* after all. I had never achieved something in my life that was so universally celebrated. Robert started using me as an example in his GMAT classes (from waitress to Harvard after taking this course!), my coworkers at the foundation seemed to regard me as more capable and perhaps smarter, and even my aunts said "Whoa" when I told them the news. My mom found a way to work my acceptance into every conversation she had (Have you met my daughter Alejandra-who-got-into-*Harvard*?). When a white package with a crimson crest arrived in the mail, I ripped it open blissfully, running my hand over the smooth cardstock and breathing in the scent of elegant paper.

But my euphoria was short-lived. Right behind the photos of students studying on well-manicured grass were my financial-aid documents. Or I should say *document*, because there wasn't much to it. No grants, no scholarships, and no need-based accommodations. In order to attend the Kennedy School, I'd have to take out over $150,000 in student loans. Coupled with the USC loans I still hadn't paid back, going to Harvard would mean saddling myself with over $200,000 in debt. Plus interest.

I felt queasy as I stared at the tuition breakdown in my hand. It was so much money. Could I really go through with this? I had always assumed a Harvard education would rubber-stamp anyone's future prospects, but now it seemed like there was a chance it could limit mine. Would I ever be able to buy a house, or even a car, with such heavy debt? I was staying afloat with my foundation salary, but I made under $40,000 a year, which made saving impossible. When would I ever see the kind of money that would allow me to make a dent in a sum as large as $200,000?

Blindfolded Cliff Jumping. That's the best way I can think of to describe what this level of risk-taking felt like to me. While everyone must weigh and navigate some level of risk throughout life, First and Onlys are often faced with difficult choices that have astronomically high stakes. That's because it's less common for us to have safety nets (family financial support), parachutes (built-in professional networks through our families), or bungee cords (savings) to make the big leaps—like starting a business or exploring a passion project—feel more manageable, as well as to cushion the landing after any natural falls or failures. And on top of the inherent danger of jumping off a cliff, we are often doing so blindly, without any sense or expectation of upcoming obstacles as we hurtle directly toward them. We rely primarily on faith, grit, and nerve.

Going to Harvard would mean betting big on the earning potential of a future version of myself, someone I wasn't certain I was capable of becoming. Looking around my bedroom at every possession I owned in the world—my childhood four-post bed, a small television, a closet filled with clothes from discount stores—it didn't feel like I was the type of person who should be taking financial risks of epic proportions. And it didn't help that I had another perfectly great (and safer) option.

In an effort to be thorough, or out of paranoia, I had submitted business school applications into the double digits. In addition to the Kennedy School, I had also been accepted to several MBA programs, and they all came with scholarships of some kind; Harvard was the only school that didn't offer me a dime. USC had even offered me a full ride. Staying close to home in LA, attending my alma mater, and graduating with zero additional debt was an incredible—and way less risky—option. Not to mention the ultimate question: Would moving across the country to start a new school retrigger my panic attacks?

Dr. Freeman and I had been working together for nine years at this point—doing a combo of cognitive behavioral and exposure therapy. And I hadn't had a panic attack since freshman year of college. As a part of my exposure therapy, I was even flying again—on short plane rides, all under an hour—to Northern California for my job at the foundation.

But moving to Massachusetts on my own would be a huge test, and I wasn't sure how I'd do. What if I fainted at orientation (again)? Or had to drop out after a few weeks because I couldn't sit through class or take exams without hyperventilating? There were a lot of unknowns and my mom was understandably worried.

"If you go to USC, you won't owe any money," my mom said, looking over my financial-aid letter. "And then you'll be home. Close to us."

She didn't have to say the next part out loud for me to know what she was alluding to. She was thinking about my anxiety. I could see it on her face as she knitted her brow, handing the paperwork back to me. "That just seems more doable."

It was certainly more pragmatic, but my mom couldn't grasp the full picture of what a degree from Harvard could mean for someone like me. More and more, the advice I was receiving from my family felt contradictory. As is the case for many First and Onlys, my mom often encouraged me to reach for the stars. At the same time, she wanted me to stay securely and reliably close by. Her fears of the unknown seemed to surface each time I faced a critical crossroads.

When I cut back my hours waiting tables to take GMAT prep classes, my mom warned I should think twice before compromising such dependable income. Considering Harvard versus USC presented a similar conundrum. She wanted success for me, but her fears stood in direct opposition to the calculated financial risk it would take to get there, and she voiced those fears at the very moments when I sorely could have used a pep talk instead. There is a focus on the immediacy of earning money that often looms over the families of First and Onlys. It's a mindset formed in reaction to their own experiences, but the reservations they express can nevertheless feel hurtful at times.

Harvard was not just a school; to me, it represented something far greater. Yes, a world-class education, but I also viewed a Harvard degree as the single most powerful professional "validator" I could earn. As a First and Only, gaining a globally recognized credential that could serve as testimony to my potential seemed especially vital to have. It could only lead to open doors.

When I landed at USC my freshman year, I had no shorthand to ease my acceptance into elite spaces; I didn't grow up in Orange County or have a parent who was a celebrity. But now, I had an opportunity to reset the playing field. I believed that having Harvard on my résumé would legitimize my belonging in a way that my life circumstances never could. Forget social ladders; this was my seat on a rocket ship—*if* I didn't pass out in public first. I knew what I wanted to do, but could I go through with it?

On the day before the deadline to commit, my hands trembled as I reviewed the online loan documents. The amount I was borrowing was more than I'd earned in the previous five years combined. I would owe the entire cost of my tuition plus the total cost of my living expenses for two years—housing, food, books, everything. How much was I really willing to bet on myself? I had taken risks in the past, but none of them included signing a binding contract with the US Department of Education to take out federal student loans.

To ease my fears, I had come up with a contingency plan. I would attend Harvard for my MPP and then, back-to-back, attend Northwestern University's Kellogg School of Management for my MBA—a program I'd been accepted to on scholarship. By earning both degrees, I'd increase my hireability, hedging against the possibility I'd end up with a whole lot of debt and nothing to show for it.

Two years in Boston and then two years in Chicago. I was delaying my entry into the workforce, but in exchange, I'd be covering all my bases with two professional networks to source a job from. This plan felt like insurance to me. I told myself that I was being sensible.

Besides, walking away from this opportunity, and always wondering "what if," felt like the most frightening scenario of all. Somehow, I knew regret would be a million times more painful than failure. If I turned back now, how would I ever know what I was truly capable of? *You earned this,* I told myself. *If you let fear or money stop you, you will always regret it.* I took a deep breath and e-signed my name. It was official. I was going to Harvard.

Over the next few months, I packed up my entire life into five large boxes, hosted a farewell dinner party with Alma and all of my closest friends, and sold my Jeep Wrangler. Now that I had signed on the dotted line, I let my student loan debt conveniently drift to the back of my mind and got ready to move across the country.

My mom agreed to fly out to Boston with me for moral support, and to bring Monica along so we could make it into a mini family vacation. And in an effort to preempt the anxiety I was sure would surface, Dr. Freeman and I scheduled weekly therapy sessions in her living room. I was grateful for her boot camp; she understood that this move had the potential to either set me free or hijack my progress.

I spent dozens of hazy afternoons lying on her couch with my eyes closed as she walked me through each second of my flight to Boston before it happened. "Now, you're walking onto the plane," she'd say gently. "You see the people ahead of you in line. Now you hear the flight attendants making announcements. Now you spot your empty seat and are walking toward it…"

I was supposed to lift one of my fingers when I felt panic coming on. Like clockwork, I'd lift my pointer finger, and she would repeat messages of calm and comfort into my open, impressionable brain. For the moment, at least, it was working.

This time around, my living arrangements were secured right away. I connected with future classmates on a Kennedy School message board during the summer, and five of us signed a lease on a powder-blue town house in Harvard Square, only a three-minute walk from school. We were all strangers, but just knowing that I wouldn't be completely alone went a long way. And I had a bottle of Xanax with three refills. I tried not to think about the very real possibility that my anxiety still might be activated by the move.

As the plane took off from LAX to Boston (my first cross-country trip in fifteen years, since my in-flight panic attack when I was eleven), I squeezed my grandmother's blue rosary in the palm of my hand, and my mom reached over to make the sign of the cross on my forehead. I prayed, *Abi be with me…Help me get through this.* Then I turned on my iPod, selected the Boston playlist I'd created to keep my mind occupied, and listened to "Boston" by Augustana. At the chorus, I closed my eyes and pretended the song was about me:

> She said I think I'll go to Boston
> I think I'll start a new life
> Where no one knows my name

Harvard Square looked exactly how it was supposed to. Historic brick buildings. Cobblestone streets. Churches with soaring spires. Charming cafés. A central park with oak and maple trees to study beneath. An underground pub serving steaming vats of rum apple cider. Crew teams rowing down the Charles River. And in the middle of it all, the iconic red-and-white Harvard T station standing prominently, announcing to a steady stream of students and tourists that they had arrived in more ways than one. Just getting off the train at that station felt thrilling.

When I walked into the Kennedy School for orientation, the first thing that caught my eye was the napkins. There was something about wiping cream cheese from my mouth using a napkin bearing Harvard's crest that seemed so intimate, like a lover reaching across the table to swipe a crumb from your face. I stood at the back of the room, watching two hundred or so graduate students mill around while balancing coffee and pastries, many already wearing brand-new Harvard sweatshirts and baseball caps. (Clearly, I wasn't the only one who had made a beeline to the bookstore upon arrival.)

I noticed a man across the room wearing a salmon-colored polo shirt with its collar popped and Sperry boat shoes, although I couldn't have named the brand at the time. I found his whole vibe charming—in a New England preppy sort of way—and started taking mental notes of the "Harvard look." Once again, my social reference points were wildly recalibrating in real time, and I didn't want to embarrass myself.

USC had taught me just how powerful a class signifier clothes could be. Yet, as is the case for many First and Onlys, these unspoken dress codes hadn't been modeled for me when I was growing up, and I didn't always realize I was breaking them until it was too late. What constituted business casual? When were you supposed to wear pantyhose? What was the proper attire for a members-only club? I'd mostly answered these questions by watching movies and TV shows. And by quickly sizing up my surroundings and then adapting on the fly. In this case, the beachy Abercrombie look of USC was out, and Vineyard Vines polo shirts were in.

When a voice over a loudspeaker announced that everyone should take their seats, I took the opportunity to snatch a few fresh napkins from the table and slip them into my book bag as souvenirs.

A couple of rows over, one of my new roommates waved at me. "Hey, thanks," I said as he motioned toward the empty seat next to him. "This is crazy, right?"

"Sure is," he said, flipping through the program. Nate was in his late twenties and looked completely in his element; his leather book bag was perfectly worn, and he'd already gone to Dartmouth. I glanced down at the sixteen-dollar pin-striped blouse I was wearing, grateful that I'd been smart enough to put more thought into my clothes this time around. *At least I know better than to wear all black again*, I thought, cringing at the memory of my first sorority rush outfit.

The head of admissions launched into her introductory remarks as a hush fell over the John F. Kennedy Jr. Forum—a meeting place known for hosting presidents, heads of state, and leaders in fields from media to business. It had been almost ten years since USC's orientation day, and I was back in a room with hundreds of peers who I was sure were more prepared than me. I was back to being the girl who had everything to lose if she didn't perform. And I was even more exposed this time around, because I had taken on so much debt.

My thoughts began to race: *Is this anxiety? What if I have another panic attack in public? What if I'm not smart enough? Look at how put-together everyone is. What if I can't keep up with my classes? What if…What if…What if…?*

Focusing on my breath, as I'd learned to do in therapy, I was struggling to corral my negative thoughts when the dean of the Kennedy School was called onto the stage.

The dean strode to the microphone with a warm smile above his salt-and-pepper beard. He was a labor economist who had cochaired a group on welfare reform for President Bill Clinton. I had never seen someone who worked for an actual US president in person before, and he might as well have been a celebrity. Sitting up in my chair, I was suddenly present—in my body and in the moment.

"Thanks, everyone," he said to a long round of applause. "Now, I know what you're all thinking," he began. "You are probably wondering if you're supposed to be here or if someone in Harvard admissions made a mistake!"

Nervous laughter erupted throughout the crowd. I glanced around at my new classmates, most of them in their twenties and thirties, and wondered if it was true. Were they all thinking the same thing I was? Now that I looked at them more closely, I had to admit they didn't seem to fit the privileged and aloof Harvard stereotype. The students around me seemed approachable and diverse, and the majority of them were dressed casually in hoodies and T-shirts.

"If that's what you're thinking right now, I want to let you all in on a little secret: Harvard. Does. Not. Make. Mistakes. If you are here, it's because you are *meant* to be. Let me say that again…Harvard does not make mistakes. So you can all relax now."

Smiles broke out across the room, and the knot in my stomach dissolved like a Chocolate Abuelita tablet in boiling milk. His logic made sense. If Harvard was the all-knowing institution I believed it to be, then by definition, that must also extend to its admissions decisions. I may not have felt confident in my own belonging yet, but I figured I could trust that Harvard knew better than I did.

With that reassurance and the advantage of having roommates to walk around with, I made it through orientation day without passing out. Then I went and shopped for books at the Harvard Coop and sat through my first week of classes without incident. I was even sleeping through the night. These things may not sound all that impressive, but to me, each tiny (Xanax-free) victory signaled that I was on my way to overcoming panic disorder for good. Feeling encouraged, I threw myself into life at the Kennedy School, and turns out, I loved it.

Cambridge was an intellectual candy shop. Popping in to Peet's Coffee in the Square, I'd overhear students discussing everything from refugee law to the midterm elections—at eight o'clock in the morning. Class debates spilled out onto the streets for happy hour. People signed up for office hours with their professors eagerly. Everyone around me seemed so inquisitive and engaged. And the discernible seasons made it feel like our time at the Kennedy School was quickly passing us by, so we'd better take advantage of it. As an LA native, I loved experiencing real weather. One of my favorite things to do was walk the two or so blocks from my house to campus in the late fall, stomping on dry leaves with a hot chocolate in hand.

Before I moved to the East Coast, I had seen real snow only a handful of times. When I was around six years old, my mom signed us up for a church trip to Santa's Village, a Christmas-themed amusement park near Lake Arrowhead in Southern California. It was a kitschy, pastel-hued wonderland, with attractions like Mrs. Claus' Kitchen, but the best part for me was that I was going to see snow for the first time. Unfortunately, my mom was just as inexperienced with cold weather as I was and forgot to pack either of us mittens, snow boots, or insulated jackets, so we spent most of that trip blowing warm air from our mouths through cupped hands onto frozen fingers.

Now I had a brand-new down coat, waterproof boots, and a town house only blocks from campus. The snow felt like a fun novelty and a good excuse to wear the scarves and beanies that had gathered dust in my LA closet. Just driving to the laundromat with my roommate, listening to the Fray while snow flurries swirled around us, felt like living in a Christmas snow globe.

During year one as an MPP student, classes were pretty straightforward—microeconomic theory, statistics, economic policy—but it was the speakers and events that blew me away. There were days when I chose between hearing a talk by Senator Ted Kennedy and having a one-on-one conversation with a member of the British Parliament. My academic advisor—whom I would drop in to see during office hours—was Pulitzer Prize winner and future United Nations ambassador Samantha Power.

But even with world-class experts wandering campus on a daily basis, what I loved the most was sitting at one of the wooden tables in the JFK Jr. Forum, where students would gather to grab a coffee or meet with their study group. I'd walk down the stairs that lined its perimeter and just take in the crowd: The nonprofit leaders, diplomats, and political operatives scattered around the room were now people to grab a sandwich with in between classes.

And the women. I was both impressed and fascinated by their remarkable backgrounds, many of them nontraditional like mine. I became fast friends with a woman named Tamara, who was born in Belgrade and immigrated with her parents to New Jersey when she was six years old. She didn't speak a word of English on her first day of public school, but by high school she was winning debate competitions. Despite the tepid encouragement of her high school guidance counselor ("I guess even snowballs have a chance in hell"), Tamara made her way to Harvard College for undergrad. She looked like some of the women I'd known in USC's Greek system—blond and often turning up in four-inch heels—but she had already worked for the Kofi Annan International Peacekeeping Training Centre in Ghana when we met.

And there were many others. A group of us gravitated toward each other, and before long we were a little squad—Tamara and me, plus Theresa (the first in her family to go to college, who went on to serve as a lieutenant in the US Coast Guard), and Ingrid (a Yale undergrad from Houston, whose family was from Mexico). It occurred to me that maybe I'd finally found my tribe—they were First and Onlys too, each driven in their own way. Whether we were meeting for brunch over mimosas at UpStairs on the Square or for hot chocolate at Burdick's, I felt a sense of belonging like never before.

When it came to academics, though, I wasn't so sure. I was used to earning good grades in high school and at USC, but now I was up against classmates with a daunting knowledge of political philosophy and foreign policy. Mostly, I sat in the back of the lecture halls, taking notes, while students in the front rows rattled off political theory with ease. I had no way of telling if I was doing well in my classes or falling behind. Since most grades were weighted to final papers and exams, the ultimate gauge would come at the end of first semester.

The day grades were posted, nerves woke me while the sky was still dark. I reached over for my laptop—which I'd made a point to sleep next to—and punched in my student ID number. I wasn't sure what to hope for. A's? Just to pass? It wasn't a feeling I'd ever had in school before.

My grades popped up on the screen, and I quickly scanned and rescanned for D's, F's, or incompletes. They weren't there. I'd done well. Certainly on par with everyone else. I exhaled a rush of air, like a balloon deflating; I hadn't realized I was holding my breath. *Okay, I've got this,* I thought, nodding.

And then, as my reassurance turned into pride, I sat up a bit straighter in bed. *I've. Got. This.*

Smiling to myself, I put on my robe and walked to the kitchen to make breakfast. I started to trust myself more after that. I may not have been able to rattle off John Locke quotes like some of my classmates, but I was keeping up just fine.

———

One afternoon in the spring, I was lying on my twin bed, reading a case study, when I realized that it had been a long time since I'd thought about my anxiety or taking Xanax. In fact, I wasn't even carrying the pillbox in my book bag anymore. It hit me that I'd made the right decision to push my limits, to move across the country, and even to take on so much student loan debt. I felt freed from the grip of anxiety and happier than I had ever been. And with real distance from my family for once, there was now space (and permission) to prioritize myself.

Geography had created emotional boundaries with my family, something I had previously struggled to establish and enforce—as can sometimes be the case for First and Onlys. Without the daily play-by-play of everyone's problems, I no longer felt like I needed to swoop in and rescue. For the first time since the ill-fated Paris trip I took with my mom, I drifted to sleep imagining all the faraway places I wanted to travel to.

As was a Kennedy School tradition, during spring break there were multiple student-led international trips planned, including to the Middle East. In undergrad, and ever since, I had used every excuse in the book to turn down invitations to travel with friends. A long weekend in Cabo? No, thanks, I'd said—I had other plans. Now, I couldn't get on a plane fast enough.

I signed up for a trip to Israel and the West Bank, jointly led by some of our Israeli and Palestinian classmates. Over a two-week period, a dozen or so of us spent half our time in Israel—visiting with politicians at the Knesset, touring an Israel Defense Forces base, and touring the Church of the Holy Sepulchre within the Old City of Jerusalem. Then our Israeli classmates dropped us off at a military checkpoint into the West Bank, where we spent the remaining week.

We crossed on foot, dragging our suitcases in the dirt road, past soldiers holding automatic weapons. Waiting for us on the other side were our Palestinian classmates and a bus that took us to the presidential palace, through an active refugee camp, and on a tour of the divided city of Hebron.

We had studied the Israeli-Palestinian conflict at school, but as I checked into my hotel room inside an ornate palace in Ramallah (for under twenty dollars a night), I thought about what a difference it was making to have an on-the-ground perspective. It had been less than a year since I'd arrived in Cambridge, and already my frame of reference about the world—and my mindset about my potential place in it—was drastically shifting.

At the Kennedy School, even the things we did for fun looked wildly different than what I was used to. Sure, there were still theme parties and bar crawls, but instead of centering our social calendar around Pac-10 football games or watching the *MTV Movie Awards*, we planned our keggers around the political calendar. And in an act of divine timing, I was entering my second year studying public policy in 2007—during one of the most extraordinary presidential election cycles in American history.

I had never felt a sense of agency when it came to politics. My family had immigrated to the US just a few years before I was born, and I don't think we ever discussed elections when I was growing up. There were definitely no exchanges around the dinner table about voting. With everyone on different schedules and working long hours, I don't remember us sitting down together at the dinner table at all. My family's focus was on keeping afloat each day, and the fate of politicians in Washington, DC, or even locally, just didn't seem consequential or relevant.

As a teenager in LA in the early '90s, I had seen Prop 187 through the lens of activism. I joined the marching in the streets and pinned a NO ON 187 button on my backpack, still too young to vote at the time. But either way, I didn't feel like there was a place for me in the political process, at any meaningful level at least.

Sitting in the JFK Jr. Forum as I watched the 2008 presidential debates with dozens of my classmates changed all that. There was nothing out of reach or inaccessible about it. We ate popcorn and drank beer. We cheered and shouted at the television as if we were watching Trojan football, especially since the candidates were debating the same policy issues we were wrestling with in class. More importantly, I listened intently to what the candidates were saying, and—newer to me—I considered whether or not I agreed with them, weighing my own opinion as a factor actually worthy of consideration.

During the first Democratic primary debate, at South Carolina State University in April of '07, I found myself increasingly drawn to then senator Barack Obama. He spoke of a "new kind of politics" and "organizing ordinary people to do extraordinary things." For someone who had always felt on the outskirts of politics, I was surprised by how deeply I connected with his words. When he referred to his campaign as a "movement" to change healthcare, education, and energy, I stared up at the screen attentively. I'd never been provoked by a political speech before, and it felt like a magnet was pulling me toward something. Exactly what, I wasn't sure yet.

I narrowed my focus during my second year at the Kennedy School, seeking out classes on political advocacy and building power in communities. I was determined to make the most of the time I had left—participating in a mock congressional campaign; singing Selena's version of "Tú, Sólo Tú" at the Kennedy School Talent Show, accompanied by MIT's mariachi band; and editing a policy journal. At the same time, I was refreshing political news online throughout the day, as the Democratic field of candidates shrank. I had never paid such close attention to an election—following the primaries, the debates, the polling.

Obama, a First and Only as the *Harvard Law Review*'s first Black president, was shattering expectations by embarking on his own version of Blindfolded Cliff Jumping. And his jump was off the highest peak in the world. I was inspired at both a professional and a personal level. It felt like he and I—and millions of the other first-generation young people who shared his self-identified "audacity of hope"—were kindred spirits.

By the spring of '08, my last semester of graduate school, it was looking increasingly likely that Obama would win the Democratic nomination for president. And then right around my graduation day, he did.

My mom and Monica hadn't returned to Boston since they'd chaperoned my move two years earlier, in their roles as human security blankets. What a difference those years had made. They arrived a few days before graduation to find me in my element. I introduced them to my friends and took them to Darwin's for the best sandwiches in Cambridge, then to Faneuil Hall for heaping lobster rolls.

Commencement brought together every graduating student in Harvard Yard—a crimson sea of thousands—

although the Kennedy School's section was far away from the center of the action. We had all been handed inflatable globes on the walk over, as a nod to our focus on policy. Even though I couldn't see the stage over the countless rows of students in caps and gowns—or hear much of anything that our graduation speakers were saying—I sat there beaming, with the world in my hands. A part of me had always lived on high alert, waiting for the next shoe to drop, yet it felt emboldening that no one could take my Harvard degree away from me now. No matter what happened, how down on my luck I might be, who or what I might lose, this was forever mine. It was as close to a personal safeguard as I had come to in my life.

After the ceremony, we went back to take a photo in the Forum, in the same spot where the dean had spoken those encouraging words to us on orientation day. When my mom handed me a bouquet of long-stemmed roses, I felt a wave of guilt. Pale pink and tied with a matching bow, they were stunning but likely expensive. My mom had spent money that she didn't have on extravagant flowers, in addition to the flight and the hotel room, because of me. It was a familiar feeling—rooted in the worry of how stretched thin she must be moneywise. But before my guilt could escalate, I pulled myself back. *This is a big deal*, I said to myself. *This will pay off. Enjoy your flowers.*

I had one summer before I'd start all over again at Northwestern's Kellogg School for my MBA, and I knew exactly how I wanted to spend it: helping to elect Barack Obama as president. It had never crossed my mind to work on a political campaign, and I had an offer for a well-paying summer internship, but after two years of watching the movement he had spoken about take shape, I had become a true believer. Apparently, so were thousands of other young people across the country. Finding an "in" when I had no previous experience was not going to be easy.

I asked every person I could think of if they had any contacts within the Obama campaign. I flew to DC to trudge around in the swampy June heat in a suit for (mostly) fruitless coffee meetings with various Hill staffers and think tank leaders who had been recommended by Kennedy School classmates.

"Tell me about yourself," a Latino politico asked me over coffee at the Hay-Adams hotel.

I launched into my background and explained why I wanted to work on the campaign, yet only a few minutes in, I detected a look in his eyes that I knew all too well. He thought I was naive. I kept going, thinking I could talk my way into a position, but the coffee ended the way I'd feared it would.

"Well, it's pretty impossible to get in right now. I'll let you know if I hear anything, though."

He was perfectly polite but clear: No one knew of any open positions, given that pretty much everyone was clamoring to join the campaign.

Then, after days of similar meetings, my last DC coffee paid off. A friend of a friend of a classmate said that he *might* know of an opportunity at the campaign headquarters in Chicago—*if* I was willing to fly myself out there immediately and work unpaid. I had just spent the last of my Harvard loan money, my student health insurance had expired, and I had under $100 in my checking account. But I also had a credit card, a $15,000 limit, and certainty in my gut that Obama was a once-in-a-lifetime leader. That was enough for me. I said I was in. A week later, I was on a flight to Chicago.

———

I landed at O'Hare with one suitcase's worth of clothes and a promise that I would be set up with "supporter housing," which is when a supporter of a campaign opens up a bedroom in their home to a staffer in need. There *was* a position for me, but I still had no idea what I'd be doing. Despite all that, I knew I'd made the right decision the moment I walked into the skyscraper on Michigan Avenue that housed the Obama campaign's headquarters.

The towering building, the expectant elevator ride, the fevered energy once I walked in—it felt like my life had shifted into some sort of higher vibrational frequency. Even the iconic red, white, and blue campaign logos scattered around the walls seemed to be in Technicolor. I had only seen this type of choreographed intensity in movies about Wall Street or busy newsrooms. There was an actual hum to the room, as dozens of hands typed decisively on laptops and multiple phone calls took place at once.

I reported to the operations cubicle, where a young woman who looked no older than twenty gave me an access badge to enter the building and the private floor, pointed out the restrooms, and assigned me a chair among packed cubicles and communal tables. I was surprised to see that, with the exception of the most senior-level staff, the average age of my new coworkers appeared to be early to midtwenties.

No sooner had I taken my seat than my new supervisor proposed we go down to the café on the ground floor to discuss my position. I was determined to be a fast learner and brought my laptop to jot down my responsibilities, which included making calls and tracking support related to gaining the national Latino vote.

Back at my desk thirty minutes later, I was just settling in when I noticed that an unknown number had been calling my cell phone nonstop. The last thing I wanted to do was excuse myself to make a phone call during my first hour on the job, but whoever it was had already left three voicemails. What if my mom or Monica had been in an accident?

Slipping into a noisy hallway as staffers hurried by, I cupped my cell phone to my ear and played one of the messages.

"Miss Campoverdi, it's Visa Fraud Alert calling. We've noticed some unusual activity on your account. Can you please give us a call back as soon as possible?"

I froze. Did I have my purse? Yes, it was on the floor under my desk. But what about my *wallet*?

I raced back to my seat and opened my purse. It was empty. Someone must have snatched the wallet out of my bag while it hung on the back of my chair at the café. And whoever stole it hadn't wasted any time, spending thousands of dollars on electronics and clothes at stores on Michigan Avenue within minutes. The good news was that

I wasn't liable for any of their purchases. The bad news? That credit card was my *only* way to pay for anything, from food to toothpaste. The balance in my checking account was five dollars now, and the replacement card they were sending wouldn't arrive for three to five business days.

I felt my face get hot when I realized that I didn't even have enough money to pay the fare for the L train ride home that evening. But not wanting to appear distracted to my new boss, I told myself I'd figure it out later and opened my laptop to work.

As the end of my first day on the campaign neared, I started going through my options: I could sleep at the office (not going to happen). Or I could ask my new boss or table-mates for twenty dollars (utterly humiliating). Someone who grew up with a secure relationship to money might not have been fazed by asking to borrow twenty bucks. But I was self-conscious about appearing to be broke and needy; it felt shameful asking anyone for a handout.

Then I remembered. One of my former Kennedy School classmates had also taken a job on the campaign. If he happened to be in the office, I might actually get through this with my dignity intact.

—*Hey Cody, are you at headquarters?*

I typed into the Messenger-style app that campaign staff used for quick communication. Hitting SEND, I prayed that he would see my message.

Excruciating minutes passed with no reply as the office thinned out fast. Soon, my options would be even more limited. Suddenly, a small chat box popped up on my screen.

—Hey! Yes I'm here! Are you?

My heart jumped. I was saved.

—Yes! I'm so sorry to ask but can I borrow $20? My wallet was stolen and I have no cash to get home :(

I couldn't afford to beat around the bush.

—Of course! But first, you have to come out to drinks with us. On me.

Sitting at a bar with Cody and his friends after being robbed was not the way I'd thought my first day would end. After one glass of wine, I was so emotionally and physically spent that I thanked him for the drink and grabbed my empty purse to leave.

"Oh, wait. Here," he said, generously handing me forty dollars, likely unaware that I'd been awkwardly waiting around for him to remember.

The whole day had been a brutal reality check—as if I needed any more—that for me and for many First and Onlys, the stakes continued to be sky-high. There was little room for error, or even happenstance.

In the days that followed, and once my replacement credit card arrived, I was able to settle into a routine at the office, if there is such a thing on a political campaign. I'd ride the L train for an hour into the city from the suburbs (where I slept in the basement of the state senate president's home), and did whatever tasks I was asked to do, which could include researching online, pitching Spanish-language radio stations, or creating media lists for the campaign.

The other young people around me were motivated, ambitious, and dedicated—working with absolute certainty that we were about to change the entire world. It was infectious. Many of them had been staffers on various political campaigns or on the Hill for years, and I became sensitive to the need to prove I belonged yet again—as with the cholas in high school, the sorority girls at USC, and the whiz kids at Harvard. World jumping was unintentionally becoming my norm. It was taxing and disorienting, but as a First and Only, it was the only way I knew how to be.

It helped that there was a growing sense of family and camaraderie among campaign staffers, fostered by long hours and a shared objective. Lengthy summer days at the campaign offices were followed by drinks with coworkers at Chicago dive bars. We'd let off steam on the weekends by playing Boston's "More Than a Feeling" on *Rock Band*. The air of possibility all around me made filling out spreadsheets feel practically profound. After my credit card fiasco, I'd begun buying Subway's $5 footlongs to limit my food spending—eating half the sandwich for lunch and half for dinner. Yet even as the balance on my credit card crept to five digits, I was certain that I was exactly where I was supposed to be.

As September rolled around, I felt crushed at the thought of leaving the campaign. Although it had always been my plan to go to Kellogg in the fall, it now seemed unimaginable. We were in the final homestretch to Election Day in November, and this was when every call, email, and outreach to the community counted the most. It was hard to reconcile my loyalty to the campaign with the fact that I had a sure thing waiting for me. An MBA on scholarship, job recruiters from the top consulting and banking firms already reaching out, and a signed lease with room-mates for an apartment in Evanston, the Chicago suburb where Northwestern's main campus is located. Plus, I had a mountain of student loan and credit card debt.

I was about to turn twenty-nine, and it was looking like I'd run out of runway to keep blindly following my passions. That was a privilege reserved for those who could afford it, and I was the definition of *tapped out*. There are people who can't fail; I wasn't one of them.

I floated through my last day in the office, feeling numb and detached. The people around me were carrying on as always—typing away on their laptops, taking phone calls in any private corner they could find, and pouring enormous mugs of coffee in the kitchen. I, on the other hand, felt like a deserter.

"I heard it's your last day," a voice said as I poured hot water into my teacup.

Looking up, I recognized a woman in her midtwenties from a few cubicle rows over.

"Are you heading out to one of the states?"

"Um, no," I said, feeling my cheeks flush. "I'm starting business school."

"Oh," she said, raising her eyebrows with genuine surprise. No one left a campaign two months before Election Day.

I wanted to explain to her that it had been a plan I'd committed to three years before and that I didn't want to go but felt like I had no choice. Instead, I said nothing, because I was certain if I said any of those things, I'd start to cry.

"Good luck."

She gave a half-hearted smile, and I did the same, walking back to my desk as my throat tightened.

Win or lose, we had all been in this together—an optimistic fight for something bigger than ourselves. But now, I had to leave. Otherwise, ending up broke and unemployed with no MBA six months after graduating from the Kennedy School was an actual possibility. It seemed so unfair, and yet it was becoming predictable at the same time. As a First and Only, my experience had shown that each new door that opened brought with it an even-higher reciprocal risk to calibrate. It seemed to never end.

When it was time to go, I said goodbye to my boss and my tablemates and packed up my laptop for the last time. It crossed my mind as I stood to leave that some other person would soon be sitting in my chair, no doubt ecstatic to have the opportunity. Who would that be? How would they feel on election night while I watched it on TV?

I still had to turn in my access badge before I left, and I decided to take the long route, through the other side of the office floor. I never went over there, mostly because it was out of the way and there were closer routes to the bathroom and elevators, but also because it was where the seniormost campaign staff worked. My heart was pounding as I gripped the hard plastic badge between my fingers and slow-walked past the glass-walled offices that held some of the political minds I most looked up to.

I was worried that I might get in trouble for being there, but when I looked around, not one person seemed to have noticed me. This was it. My last chance to steal a glance at the genius architects of the Obama campaign before accepting that I'd soon be back on the outside looking in. I picked up my pace, searching every inch of the space with my eyes. And then, defeated, I kept going toward the exit. As fate would have it, the offices were all empty.

Making my way to the operations cubicle near the front entrance, I handed in my badge—aware that I now couldn't come back to the campaign offices even if I wanted to. The same young woman who'd first given it to me smiled and wished me good luck.

"Thanks," I croaked, my throat stiff and dry.

I tried hard to hold myself together as I tapped repeatedly for the elevator down. Thankfully, there was no one inside when it arrived. As soon as the doors closed, I burst into tears.

Like a good soldier I pushed through, and over the next few days I took a one-way train to Evanston, registered for classes, bought my course books, and settled into my new life as a business school student vying for a job at Goldman Sachs or McKinsey. The idea of working at either place wasn't appealing, but I told myself that enough was enough. This was what I *had* to do in order to stabilize my life, provide for my family, and be practical for once. This was what it looked like to be *responsible* and to accept that helping to elect Obama as president was just not in the cards. I told myself that I was ready to learn some accounting.

Two weeks into fall semester, I was 100 percent sure that I had made the biggest mistake of my life.

You know the swimming-pool game Marco Polo, where one person closes their eyes and flails around blindly in the water while listening for the proximity of the voices around them to forecast whether they are getting "hotter" to or "colder" from their target? Every day that I was in business school felt like a game of Marco Polo, as my own inner voice faded softer and softer, and I felt farther away from where I was supposed to be. I sat through finance classes unable to shake the nagging feeling that I'd made a wrong turn and that the window of opportunity to course-correct was rapidly closing. There was no question that I was lucky to be at one of the nation's top business schools, but in my heart, I knew that it wasn't my path.

Common sense, reason, and security all pointed toward staying put. I already had homework, and rent was coming due. The alternative meant going back to living off my credit card and attempting to return to a position that would definitely end on November 4, even if we *won* the election. But there was logic, and then there was my gut. And my gut was screaming at me.

Knowing that anyone I asked for advice would likely try to stop me, I didn't share my plans. Instead, I made an appointment with the head of admissions with one objective: to drop out of business school.

"I don't know how to say this, but I need to leave Kellogg and go back to the Obama campaign," I told her.

Her serious expression as I fidgeted with my hands revealed no reaction whatsoever. Was I ruining my life?

"I feel horrible for taking a spot in the class, and I'm hoping you can find someone to take my place. The truth is, my heart is with the campaign."

An elegant Black woman in a skirt suit, the admissions director listened intently as I talked her through my reasoning. She seemed to soften a bit, nodding as I shared why I believed in Obama so much.

"I understand how you could feel that way, so I'm going to figure out how to free you from your commitment," she said finally. "This is unorthodox, and normally I would respond very differently. But I recognize that we are in a unique moment in time."

It was as if a heavy weight on my chest had suddenly been lifted. I could breathe again.

"Also, we won't hold you responsible for paying back all of your tuition from the past few weeks or for the remaining two years."

I was startled. It hadn't even occurred to me that I'd signed legal documents committing to be responsible for the entire cost of my tuition and scholarships. There was no way I would've been able to drop out of business school if I'd still had to pay for an MBA I wouldn't get.

Now, with Kellogg's blessing, I quickly called the campaign, asking to come back in any capacity. The answer was yes. I was back at the campaign office working on outreach to various constituency groups by the following week.

I don't want to make any of this sound easy. It was a huge Blindfolded Cliff Jump, especially for someone with no safety net. This time around, I was assigned a seat right outside the men's restroom, which didn't make for the best eat-at-your-desk conditions. I sat in that chair all day, only getting up to stretch when my back started aching from not moving. My eyes were fatigued from staring at spreadsheets, and my right eye started twitching at random times.

But none of that mattered. Every task, phone call, and

spreadsheet, no matter how minor, felt meaningful. And when Obama himself held a conference call with campaign staff in the final weeks before Election Day, he urged us—in the way only he could—to stay the course, keep working, and dare to believe. So I did. Not once did I question my decision to leave Kellogg, and not once did I wish I was anywhere else in the world.

On election night in Chicago's Grant Park, I stood awestruck in the staff area, watching President-elect Barack Obama take the podium for his victory speech as an enormous crowd cheered. Looking across hundreds of thousands of people in every direction, I took in everything about the scene, certain that it would be one of the most significant of my life—the way the air smelled like fresh grass, the twinkling lights of the Chicago skyline, the tears streaming down faces all around me.

"I was never the likeliest candidate for this office," Obama declared to the crowd.

I and other First and Onlys understood what that was like. We understood what it had meant that he did it anyway. His win illustrated "Yes, we can" to us on so many different levels.

I cried my own happy tears as he called on us to "reclaim the American Dream," and in that moment, anything felt possible.

When the rally ended, the celebration burst onto the streets, flooding every L stop, sidewalk, and corner with ecstatic faces, hollering, and honking cars. It was a collective expression of joy on a scale that was breathtaking to witness.

The next day, the sobering reality hit.

While our country had a new president-elect, I now owed $16K in credit card debt and six figures in student loans, and I had no apartment, no health insurance, no car, no job, and no cash. None of these things were a surprise, of course, but I had pushed it all out of my mind during the campaign. Now, with no place to report to in the morning, I couldn't ignore how far out on a limb I'd gone. I was living on borrowed time (and money).

Other than senior White House staff, no one seemed to know for sure if they'd have a job come Inauguration Day, particularly young campaign staffers. And no one seemed to know what the process was to find one. There was an unspoken distaste for anyone who was seen as maneuvering for a job before Election Day, but now that we'd won, all anyone could talk about was joining the Obama administration. "Do you know what you're going to do now?" people asked each other, wondering as much for themselves as for the other person. After all, thousands of staff, volunteers, and interns from across the country had worked on the campaign, and there wouldn't be enough administration jobs to go around.

I knew so little about how Washington worked at the time, but I wanted nothing more than to be a part of creating the change Obama spoke of. A job in the actual White House seemed like a total impossibility for me, yet I would've been happy with any position in the administration. I heard whispers that most junior-level positions would be figured out at the last minute. This was how it always worked, my campaign friends said. There would be a famine over the next few months during the transition, and then a feast in the final days leading up to inauguration. "You could just go to DC and wait it out," they told me.

After everything I'd already put on the line, it didn't seem like the craziest idea. So I opened up another credit card account, with a $10,000 limit this time, and booked a one-way flight to Washington.

On the surface, I must've seemed like I was riding high. My Kennedy School friends, and even some former Kellogg classmates, congratulated me for making the decision to go back to the campaign. I flew home to LA for the holidays, and my mom threw me a big party to toast my triumphant return after two and a half dizzying years away. Everyone wanted to know if I'd met Obama (I had not) and if I'd been to the White House (nope). But I knew the truth: I was still in a do-or-die scramble. Just a fancier-looking one.

I tried not to think about the fact that there was no plan B as I flew to DC in January. When I was overwhelmed as a child, Abi used to tell me, "One step at a time...one foot in front of the other," so I told myself to concentrate only on the very next step—getting to Washington. It was how I'd learned to tolerate—and even become comfortable with—ambiguity, a skill that First and Onlys often develop out of necessity. My boyfriend at the time (whom I'd met on the campaign) offered to let me temporarily crash at his place while I tried to find a job, and although I wasn't sure where our relationship or my life was heading, I was choosing to be hopeful about both.

My campaign friends were right about the famine. Weeks went by during which my résumé was supposedly being passed around for consideration, but I heard absolutely nothing. Each day, the countdown to inauguration grew more deafening. There was wall-to-wall news coverage analyzing what to expect in President Obama's first one hundred days, high-level appointments were being announced, and many of my campaign friends were locking down jobs. There was no distracting myself. I tried to act unbothered, but inside I was a bundle of nerves, refreshing my inbox constantly.

And then one day, no more than a week before inauguration, an interview request came in by email from the White House Office of Intergovernmental Affairs for an assistant position. And then another similar one from the White House Office of Legislative Affairs. "Oh my God," I stammered with both hands pressed over my mouth. This was my shot.

Days later, I was in the middle of one of my interviews at the Presidential Transition Office when a striking Black woman in her early forties with wavy shoulder-length hair stuck her head in the room and asked if she could speak to me for a moment.

"I promise I'll bring her right back," she said, with a friendly smile, to the person interviewing me.

I followed the woman into another room, and she introduced herself as Mona, the incoming White House deputy chief of staff for policy.

"I saw your résumé, and I wanted to speak to you about potentially being my special assistant," she said casually, like it wasn't the most exciting thing I'd ever heard.

We spent some time talking through my background, the job, and her expectations, and it became immediately clear that we had a great natural flow and rapport with each other. It was obvious right off the bat that she was no-nonsense and whip-smart yet completely down-to-earth.

"Okay, so…would you like the job?" she said, catching me completely off guard.

I couldn't believe what was happening. I'd be working for a woman of color who managed policy in President Obama's White House? To say it was a dream would imply I could've ever imagined it for myself, and this was beyond any hope I'd had.

"Yes, I would," I said quickly, before she could change her mind.

"Fabulous. We'll be in touch soon with next steps," she said, walking me to the door.

As I rode the Metro back to my boyfriend's apartment, I looked around with new eyes. There was the young, disheveled Hill intern across the aisle, reading a book. A lobbyist-looking man in a suit, holding on to the handrails. And then there was me. A soon-to-be White House staffer who may have taken an unconventional road to DC but had arrived all the same. This would now be home.

Not long after, I received an email from the Transition Office instructing me to report to work early in the morning on January 21, 2009.

A.k.a. the Obama administration, day one.

This time in my life was defined by a series of all-or-nothing decisions I made with no fallback plan, what I've been referring to as Blindfolded Cliff Jumping. It's easy in retrospect to see how they all fit together, but the choices I made could've been disastrous; things could've easily gone in the other direction. And that's the point. As First and Onlys, the risks we must often take to level up in our lives and careers have high stakes, are daunting, and can even seem foolish.

Each time I came to a critical crossroads, I had no frame of reference or reassurance that what I was experiencing was typical or predictable. I'd seen First and Onlys on *Forbes* lists, on the Time 100: Most Influential People list, and highlighted on social media, yet despite sometimes briefly nodding to difficult childhood circumstances, the write-ups didn't include many details about what it *really* took for them to achieve their successes. Their paths seemed smoother and less twisty than mine. I often wondered what I was doing wrong.

They say if you can't see it, then you can't be it. But that concept doesn't only apply to the successes. It also applies to the calculated perils, pitfalls, and plunges. If we can't see the nosedives of others, it's harder to steel ourselves against the terror of our own.

When I moved to DC without a promise or a lead, it would've meant the world to be reassured that I was not a fool. That I was, in fact, doing what First and Onlys must often do—operating purely on raw instinct. I was rewarded when I trusted my gut, but it was scarier than it needed to be. No one had validated to me how extraordinarily

important it is for someone who is first gen to hone and follow their intuition. That our inner knowing can, in fact, be
wise. Any confirmation to that effect would've made all my
Blindfolded Cliff Jumping over the previous years—taking
on debt to go to Harvard, joining the campaign, dropping
out of business school, moving to DC—feel far less rash.

After living in survival mode for as long as I could
remember, I was convinced that I'd now reached a highland
of sorts. I had gone from Gladstones to the White House in
under five years. I was sure it was the apex where I could
catch my breath, if only for a moment.

I was wrong.

CHAPTER EIGHT

EVERLONG

THERE'S NOTHING LIKE the FBI digging into every inch of your past to trigger a good old-fashioned case of impostor syndrome.

I found out on my first day at the White House that I'd need Top Secret security clearance in order to do my job. Since I was working directly for a deputy chief of staff, I'd have access to sensitive national security documents on a daily basis. That meant I'd have to be rigorously vetted; in other words, the FBI would be examining my entire life up until that point.

No detail was too small. I had to list every place I'd ever lived, every job I'd ever had, personal information about my family, physical health, mental health, medications, boyfriends, friends, you name it. And for each of these, I also had to supply the names of several people who could corroborate that what I was saying was true. I took care while filling out the 127-page SF86 questionnaire with over twenty-six different sections; my colleagues had warned that it was better to overshare than to withhold.

If the FBI found out you were hiding anything, even the smallest detail, you were toast, they'd said.

Going all the way back to birth, I laid out the step-by-step map of my life. It felt like a flip-book of the most personal, and judgeable, parts. The food stamps, my family's complicated immigration story, my father's missing whereabouts and questionable dealings, the anxiety medication I had taken (doses included), the therapists I'd seen, the embarrassing jobs I took to make a buck, the modeling gigs—it all had to be in there. There was an entire section about my father and his family history that I had no choice but to leave mostly blank. They even asked me to share anything unseemly or humiliating I had experienced, as well as the amount of financial debt I carried. It was how the FBI would figure out if I was a blackmail risk—by looking under every stone in my past.

Am I the kind of person the FBI will want to sit ten steps from the Oval Office? I wondered as I checked the box admitting to having taken benzodiazepines.

Don't get me wrong; I wasn't ashamed of my upbringing, decisions, struggles, or life. But I was also realistic that people with my background weren't the typical inhabitants of 1600 Pennsylvania Avenue. Sure, I wasn't a well-born heir apparent to a political dynasty, but I wasn't even a girl with two parents, a middle-class upbringing, and summers spent on the lake. I was terrified that who I was *could*, and *would*, be held against me. The full scope of my "impostor-ness" was about to be lit up with floodlights in front of the federal government.

It didn't help that all this was happening on the heels

of the *Maxim* mess, when I was feeling especially fragile, exposed, and stupid. I'd already experienced the cruel reality that sometimes the choices you make in your Lonely Hustle phase can be weaponized against you in the future. The early lives of First and Onlys don't always clean up well, and I felt pretty sure I'd compromised my career over the course of a four-hour photo shoot six years earlier.

For the next eight or so months, FBI agents called or visited everyone from my next-door neighbor in the '90s to the general manager of a restaurant I briefly worked at—something I learned only after receiving several panicked phone calls from my mom. Apparently, when calling my contacts, agents didn't explain the context of their inquiry, except to say that I was a "person of interest."

And then they went silent.

It seemed like the results of my background check were taking way longer than everyone else's, which I took as a very bad sign. *Something must've gone wrong*, I thought.

I called over to the clearance office under the guise of making sure that they had everything they needed, but I was really looking for any sort of sign that I hadn't already been flagged for rejection. A few more months passed, and then I finally received word: I would receive Top Secret/Sensitive Compartmented Information security clearance.

I couldn't believe it. Top Secret was the highest level, and SCI access was a tick above that, since it required an additional screening process. It felt as if my life had been given a stamp of approval by the US government. After inspecting every inch of my background, the FBI apparently thought I was good enough. Now, I just had to believe it myself.

It reminded me of an encounter I'd had a few months into my first year at the Kennedy School. A classmate of mine was sitting alone at a table in the empty Forum. He normally carried himself with a self-assured presence, but on that day his eyes were cast down and his shoulders were a bit hunched over. I slid into the seat across from him and asked if something was wrong.

"I don't know if I belong here, you know? Back home, I was helping people in my neighborhood every day. And now, I've left everyone, and for what? There isn't anyone else like me at this place," he said. He had been the first person from his working-class family to go to college, let alone graduate school.

I was taken aback by his confession, though perhaps I shouldn't have been. I'd heard a variation of the same theme from other First and Onlys throughout the years. I was beginning to realize that there was a lot more to the concept of impostor syndrome than I'd previously thought. By any measure, my classmate was one of the highest achievers in his community and he didn't lack confidence.

The term *impostor phenomenon* was coined by two psychologists in the late 1970s, in a paper exploring the "internal experience of intellectual phoniness" of high-achieving women. Since the beginning, impostor syndrome (as it's now more commonly called) was explored as an experience that happened *inside* a person because of their *own* feelings of inadequacy, regardless of their success. Through time, the phrase began to be lobbed at not only women, but also First and Onlys and people of color. I remember being warned by teachers that I might develop impostor syndrome—and then blaming myself for not being more confident.

Yet something critical went missing in my early understanding of impostor syndrome—and in the way we are often introduced to the concept as young people. The conventional definition implies that there is something wrong with *us*, which only exacerbates any stories we might be telling ourselves about not being good enough. But how about the ways in which our *external* environments give rise to our feelings of inadequacy? Wouldn't *any* person—no matter how self-assured they are—experience legitimate feelings of estrangement in the same situation, when confronted by social systems that disadvantage them and favor the privileged and connected individuals who control them? It's not just impostor syndrome; it's Impostor Syndrome Plus.

I once saw a cartoon that depicted a race between people of color and white people (although the analogy can apply to other First and Onlys too). All the runners are lined up next to each other at the starting line, yet in the lanes with people of color, there are various obstacles on the path to the finish line: large boulders, a moat with an alligator, and spikes coming up from the ground. The lanes with the white runners are free and clear. In the caption, one of the white runners says to the other, "See, we are all running the same distance." If you look closely at the faces of the people of color, they're wincing in anticipation. Did the people of color have impostor syndrome? Perhaps. But didn't they also have a rational sense of foreboding that despite their comparable hard work and talent, they still might not be able to go as far or as fast?

Feelings of inadequacy don't just appear out of thin air or arise solely from our own insecurity. Self-doubt doesn't happen in a vacuum. Regardless of how confident we may feel, First and Onlys often receive subtle (and not so subtle) external messages that we are different, don't quite measure up to our peers, or are lacking in experience, exposure, or pedigree. And with each achievement, these messages tend to happen *more* often, not less. I was certainly no stranger to this dynamic. In fact, it had already played out for me during my first year at the Kennedy School.

After passing my fall classes and feeling more at home in Cambridge, I was starting to feel pretty confident about the whole Harvard thing. So when I heard that there was a competitive leadership course offered only during the winter term that other students called "life-changing," I was eager to sign up. The class was billed as one big social experiment meant to reveal how others see us, by allowing group members to dissect each other in a public forum, using "classroom dynamics in real time." Supposedly, that feedback would allow us to become stronger leaders.

It sounded interesting, though I did receive a warning. A friend of mine—a first gen Latina who has cerebral palsy and uses crutches as mobility devices—had previously taken the class and had a very bad experience.

"So, you're a cripple?" she remembered the professor saying to her, loudly in front of the packed room. She had asked for a seat to be held for her at the start of each class.

"No, I don't like that word," she said, shaken. "I'm a person with a disability."

The professor continued to refer to her as "crippled"

from that day on—for supposed teaching purposes—which led the rest of the class to feel emboldened to call her that as well. There was even a group analysis exercise on whether her identity was solely tied to her disability. She later filed a complaint and started therapy because of the experience.

I should've recognized the class as a tailor-made environment for calling out the "otherness" of people outside the power-and-privilege hierarchy—or simply a training camp for mob mentality. But gaining the tools to be a better leader seemed to me like exactly the kind of work I should be doing, so I enrolled in the course and prepared to "free myself to lead" (or so the syllabus claimed).

One morning during a break, I asked a classmate for his thoughts on what made a good leader. He was *that* guy in the class—the one who regularly raised his hand to challenge the professor and dominated all group discussions. He looked like he could've been an extra in the movie *Dead Poets Society*.

"Well, lots of things. The ability to motivate and inspire people," he said. "But people only listen to what *you* have to say because you dress like a slut," he added matter-of-factly.

I felt my entire body contract. *Did he just say what I think he said?*

Before I could respond, the professor called us back to our seats. As I walked to my desk, dizzy and breathing shallow, I looked down at my clothes. I was in a red-and-white plaid blazer, jeans, and boots (it was January in Boston). What was wrong with what I was wearing?

Still reeling, I raised my hand and shared with the class what had just happened. We were supposed to be deconstructing dynamics around identity, right?

Immediately, a woman in a sleek ponytail raised her arm in the air forcefully, trying to get the professor's attention.

"I used to be a model too, but you don't see *me* using my appearance for anything," the woman said, pressing her lips together for emphasis. She was a former military officer, and everyone listened closely whenever she spoke. I had always admired her—until now.

"*I'd* rather be known for my mind and my thoughts, not for my body," she said, her delivery the equivalent of a hard shove.

So would I, I wanted to shout across the classroom. I felt tears forming in my eyes as I sat there humiliated. My immediate circle of friends knew my background and that I had once worked as a model, but I'd had no idea that this was something widely known on campus. Either way, I had earned my right to be at Harvard along with the rest of them. What did the way I dressed have to do with anything?

A class discussion ensued about using one's appearance to get ahead. We're talking over a dozen hands in the air—both women and men—as gender and sexuality tropes were flung around the room, all in the name of analysis. "The type of woman who chooses her body over her brain" was a phrase that went unchecked by the professor, as if it were an either-or proposition. I looked on in silence. It was my nightmare—a room full of people dissecting my appearance and choices from a place of judgment. They weren't even talking about me anymore, but a cartoon caricature of me.

I kept waiting for the teachable moment, when the professor would show leadership himself, stop the onslaught, and reveal to us what we should be learning from the nature of the discussion. Instead, he sat back passively and didn't say a word. No boundary setting, no reframing, no circling back to point out the implicit bias that had taken over the classroom. Class ended, and all I took with me was shame. Had everyone really been seeing me through that lens all this time? I hadn't felt like an impostor in grad school before, but now I sure did. It was like Mike Wallace judging me when I was a child all over again.

A few years later, the woman who was the ringleader that day was publicly exposed on the front page of every newspaper for having a scandalous extramarital affair with a four-star general whose biography she was writing, granting her access to national security documents she wouldn't have had access to otherwise. That ended up being the big takeaway for me—that some people speak in projections, ultimately saying more about themselves than about you.

But in the moment, her words destroyed me, because back then I took all the shaming so personally. I was still coming to terms with the magnitude of sexist resistance women face when they embody any level of multidimensionality. How uncomfortable it makes others when women don't fit neatly into one archetypal box. How when that's the case, society often chooses our box *for* us, regardless of how we see ourselves. And it's usually the most clichéd one, not allowing for complexity, contradiction, or even our own humanity.

It was true I didn't have a cookie-cutter background, but writing off a woman's contributions or motivations because of her appearance, clothes, or sexuality is the very height of misogyny.

And how had my being a First and Only—the choices I'd made, the choices I'd felt were available to me—factor in? Now I see how the multiple elements of my identity as a first gen woman of color came into play. I didn't feel empowered to defend myself in class because I wasn't sure that what I had done was defensible. Maybe I had cheapened myself, like they said, and I didn't belong. They were pretty much telling me that I was an impostor, as a decent woman and as a Harvard student, and who was I to contradict them? I wish I had steadied my voice and called out their toxic bias with authority. But unfortunately, I didn't understand this at the time. There would still be years more of Impostor Syndrome Plus to contend with in my future.

No one was better at beating themselves up than I was during my first year at the White House. I'd been on the job for around six months when I was contacted by a *New York Times Magazine* reporter, asking if I'd be interested in participating in a story about what it was like to be a young person in the Obama White House. The invitation gave me heartburn. After the *Maxim* revelation, I had received dozens of interview requests, and even though it would've offered me a chance to defend myself, I'd turned everything down.

As any good political staffer will tell you, becoming a distraction is the last thing you want to do and the quickest way to lose your job. Yet according to the *Times* reporter, several of my peers were already on board. After talking to my boss and clearing it with the White House press office, I agreed to an interview, telling myself that this would be a chance to start rewriting the false narrative that had taken over my Google search results.

As I sat under bright lights for the story's photo shoot, perched on the arm of a red leather chair, I was distracted by thoughts of what the reporter would write about me and whether it would ultimately make everything worse. But when the issue came out, it was mostly a story about a group of idealistic kids—humanizing, if anything. In the photo they chose, I wore a blazer buttoned to my collarbone and a knee-length skirt, as I sat alongside three colleagues that I respected. I bought two copies: one for me, one for my mom. I wanted her to see that her daughter hadn't blemished her life in an insurmountable way. That my grandmother would have had no reason to be ashamed. I started to hope that maybe I was past it all, finally.

The day after the magazine hit stands, I was sitting at my desk when I heard two young female voices right outside my door. My boss and I shared a small windowless space, nothing separating us but a partition wall, and I could hear everything that was going on in the hallway.

"Did you see that *New York Times Magazine* story?" Woman A asked, out of sight but just feet from my desk.

"Oh, yeah, I did," Woman B replied. "It's so bizarre, right?"

When I heard them mention the article, I stopped typing.

"Totally!" said Woman A. "I mean, can you believe some of the people they included in the story?"

"Well, no one actually *legitimate* wanted to do it," Woman B replied, "so there's that." They both began to laugh.

I felt sick. I could tell by how loudly they were speaking

right next to my desk that there was one intended audience: me.

They continued trashing the article. Suddenly, I couldn't sit still and listen to one more word. I burst out of my office, coming face-to-face with two of my peers.

"Oh!" Woman B said, pretending she was surprised to see me. They abruptly walked away.

It seemed that my feelings of inadequacy could not be overcome by will (or self-esteem) alone. Despite pumping myself up on the morning walk to work, a sideways glance in the afternoon would shake my confidence all over again.

Overcoming my impostor syndrome was going to take a lot more than a personal pep talk. For First and Onlys, full acceptance into social systems not meant for us often takes championing from someone at the top of the hierarchy—a signal to the larger group that we belong. I was fortunate to work in a White House that had people of color at the highest levels of power—from the president and his senior advisors to the heads of policy councils and my own boss. Yet the overarching dynamics in most systems remain the same. It tends to be white men who hold the cards to decide which First and Onlys are granted legitimacy—and therefore promotions, access, and opportunity. I felt like I needed a champion and protector, yet finding one wouldn't be something I had any control over.

The first glimmer of hope appeared at the annual White House Correspondents' Association dinner. Special assistants were sometimes invited to sit at staff tables in the back of the glitzy invitation-only gala, but I wasn't particularly optimistic that I'd make the cut. When a group of us were offered last-minute tickets, I jumped at the opportunity and took a late train to the mall to buy a formal dress at Marshalls. Held every year in a gigantic ballroom in the Washington Hilton, the correspondents' dinner was the night when DC and Hollywood collided, the highlight being a comedic speech by the sitting president. I would've been excited to be a waitress in the room, let alone sit at one of the tables.

As I squeezed my way through the noisy crowd, I passed A-list celebrities angling to speak to Washington insiders, and TV news anchors in black-tie attire. I was standing at the back of the vast ballroom, taking in the pageantry of it all, when I noticed a White House senior staff member looking over. He motioned for me to come to the front of the room, where Ben Affleck was casually chatting with a cabinet secretary. I was tempted to look over my shoulder. Was he really talking to me?

Up until that point, I wasn't sure the senior staff member even knew who I was. Cool and self-assured, Michael was a member of the inner circle of Chicago loyalists that everyone admired, as well as Valerie Jarrett's chief of staff.

"Hey, how's it going? Pretty great, right?" he said, gesturing around the room. Every person within ten feet of us was world-famous.

"Yeah, it really is," I said. Someone bumped into my back, and when I turned around to look, it was a pop star.

"I'm glad I ran into you," Michael continued. "There's something I've been wanting to say." He leaned in.

I held my breath.

"You're doing everything right. I just want you to know

that people are noticing, and you're doing everything right. Keep it up." He offered me his fist to pound.

"Thank you!" I said, meeting his fist with mine. "I will. Seriously, thank you."

I didn't know which "people" he was talking about, but it didn't matter. Simply knowing that the powers that be were watching—and approved—was a shot in the arm when I needed it the most.

I was doing it. Demonstrating that I wasn't an impostor and slowly proving my worth. Perhaps even inching one step closer to having a mentor, in addition to my boss. Mona had my back, but her protection could only go so far. At the end of our first week at the White House, she had assured me that as long as I did the work, I'd be fine. But would that still be the case if she wasn't around?

After two years together, I was about to find out, when Mona announced that she was leaving the White House. Although her impending departure would soon leave me with no job, it was comforting to know that I had done right by her, that I had met her expectations, especially since she had stood by me at my most vulnerable time.

It would've been nice if it had lasted longer, I thought. *But it was a good run.*

One thing was for sure—I was not looking forward to trying to find a new job in Washington and having to prove myself all over again.

But days later, a gray-haired senior advisor to the president approached my desk and asked if I wanted to chat about my plans for the future. Pete was known for his unmatched political experience and for being a no-nonsense straight shooter; I respected him immensely.

"So what do *you* want to do?" he said as we sat in his office. I hadn't been asked that question in a very long time.

I stalled. "What do you mean?"

"Well, you shouldn't leave the White House. You've put in your dues. What do you want to do now?"

I was floored. Open-ended opportunity was not something I was used to. I had been doing whatever it took to get to the next step—and the one after that—for over twenty years. Climbing, morphing, proving, surviving, climbing, morphing, proving, surviving. Was he really giving me the space to stop and consider what it was I actually wanted? Did I even know what that was anymore?

I looked at the photos of President Obama on the wall as I considered it. What had driven me all these years? I thought back to the empty refrigerator of my childhood, the lush green lawn of the high school we couldn't afford, the hospital hallway where I chased down my mom's distracted doctor during her cancer treatment at Kaiser, the cruel anti-immigrant signs during the Prop 187 era. I'd always been inspired by my family, my community, and anyone who had been similarly disenfranchised or disempowered.

"Well?" Pete asked, calling me back to the present moment.

"I want to do something related to the Latino community, in communications."

I could've charged ahead in any direction at that point—domestic policy, foreign policy, legislative affairs—but I wanted to go back to where I'd started. Just as I'd pulled apart the Russian nesting doll of my family's generational patterns, I wanted to remove the layers of incomplete identities I'd taken on in an effort to be accepted: perfect daughter with no needs, valiant family hero, tough wannabe chola, fun sorority girl, serious Ivy Leaguer, tireless campaign staffer, and now, stoic White House aide. I wanted to remember who I was before I started to believe that she wasn't enough.

So not long after, I stepped into my dream job— deputy director of Hispanic media. Along with the director of Hispanic media, we were the first team solely dedicated to Latino-focused communications in the White House's history. I'm confident that my promotion would not have been possible without Pete's endorsement and championing, which sent the signal that I had something worthwhile to contribute. His support was the sturdy bridge I crossed over into my own power. Once on the other side, I finally felt safe enough to show up as my authentic self. I had worked hard, and it finally sank in—I deserved to be there.

Over the next two years, I developed and carried out the White House's media strategy focusing on the US Latino community in both Spanish and English. Since all issues are Latino issues, my work touched everything—from healthcare to the economy. And I didn't feel isolated anymore. A small group of us whose work focused on Latinos started to meet regularly in the West Wing office of the seniormost Latina in the White House. Before long, Cecilia's gathering of solidarity and comradeship became a highlight of my week.

I still can't believe some of the experiences I had during my time at the White House: I toasted the passage of the Affordable Care Act from the Truman Balcony, staffed the

G20 summit in Mexico and the Summit of the Americas in Colombia, called my mom from onboard Air Force One, watched Fourth of July fireworks from the South Lawn as the Foo Fighters performed "Everlong," and rode in a presidential motorcade through Mexico City. The parts of me that had been the basis of my impostor syndrome in the past—being first gen, being Latina, growing up in challenging circumstances—had become the perspectives that were helping me to carry out my job successfully. My differences were now my superpowers.

Those qualities were what led me to be in the Oval Office with President Obama one afternoon in August 2011. He was sitting in a brown leather chair, a bust of Abraham Lincoln visible to the right of his head and a bust of Martin Luther King Jr. to the left, as I briefed him one-on-one in preparation for an interview with *Latina* magazine. Words were leaving my mouth, but my mind was on another track entirely, thinking *How did I end up sitting next to the president of the United States as he prepares to speak directly to our community?*

Minutes later, as I watched from the side of the Resolute Desk while he chatted on the phone with the reporter, I was instantly transported back to how inspired I'd felt sitting in the Kennedy School four years earlier, watching him on the big screen as he debated onstage during the primary.

But the moment I'll always treasure the most is when I had the opportunity to introduce my mom and sister to President Obama. It was a full circle that was generations in the making; I only wish Abi could've been there.

When the three of us walked into the Oval Office together and I saw the president standing there to greet us, a familiar wave of Impostor Syndrome Plus surged through my body. Had I really earned this moment? And then I stood back and saw a woman who had grown up dirt-poor in Mexico holding hands with the first Black president of the United States. They went on to chat about her experience starting a career as an inner-city public school teacher at the age of forty-five.

Was she an impostor? Was I? No, neither of us was. We belonged to a tribe of trailblazers, inherently worthy *because* of our struggles, not despite them. Our survivor skills and refusal to give up had paved our way just as much as any achievements could have, which in turn made even the hardest parts of our past feel meaningful. As the White House photographer positioned himself to take a photo, the four of us put our arms around each other warmly. That photo—now framed at my mom's house—is signed *To Cecilia, All the best...and thanks for Alejandra! Barack Obama.*

During my years at the White House, it was crucial to remind myself of the perspective I brought to the table, but my path was equally paved by the encouragement, championing, and protection of those within the power structure. These two factors fed off one another, and I found a sense of belonging in Washington because I was fortunate to experience both. In fact, the more clear-eyed I was about Impostor Syndrome Plus being both an outgoing *and* an incoming phenomenon—how we feel about ourselves *and* how we are received by the systems we are a part of—the less I felt its effect.

When after four years at the White House, I was recruited to launch a media venture focused on Latinos, I made the decision to leave with the reassurance that I was doing so on my own terms. I walked into my going-away party in the historic Diplomatic Reception Room of the EEOB and was taken aback to see it filled to the brim with colleagues who had now become good friends. My past bosses and peers took turns sharing reflections of our times together, and then I was handed a large framed photo of the president and me in the Oval, handwritten notes filling every inch of its white border. On so many levels, it was the realization of what I had prayed for during my first week at the White House.

Then I crossed into the West Wing to take my departure photo with President Obama. Before we posed in front of his desk, I took a deep breath, held both of his hands, and launched into hurriedly sharing with him through tears what I'd always wanted him to know—that the last four years had altered not only my life, but that of my family and generations of my family to come.

He squeezed my hands and beamed—an OG First and Only if there ever was one—as he nodded knowingly.

It was undeniable that my time at the White House represented a First and Only pinnacle in my life and career. The top of the highest summit I had been climbing for as long as I could remember. When I walked out of the black iron gates for the last time as a staffer, my body erupted in goose bumps. I felt proud of what I'd accomplished. Redeemed.

So I was cured now, right?

Not so fast.

CHAPTER NINE

LA TRENZA

Pᴜʟʟɪɴɢ ᴜᴘ ᴛᴏ my aunt Nannette's house in Santa Monica for Thanksgiving, two years after leaving the White
House, was like revisiting Main Street at Disneyland as
an adult. Not one blade of grass seemed to have changed
since I moved away eight years earlier, but everything now
seemed small-scale and less grand. It was the same white
farmhouse exterior, set at the corner of a quaint residential
neighborhood. The stone staircase leading up to the front
door was still in need of a facelift, and its splintered hand-
rail looked just as likely to fall over as ever.

As I struggled to balance on each step in stiletto boots,
a stack of overpriced Urth Caffé pumpkin pies in my arms,
my emotional equilibrium felt just as off-kilter. I had moved
back to LA a few months earlier, and nostalgic memories
of climbing these same stairs on Thanksgiving over the
last twenty-plus years came roaring through me: carrying baby Monica in a car seat up the steps, giving old boyfriends the lowdown as they prepared to meet my family,
feeling grown-up because it was always assumed that I'd

sit at the adults' table for dinner while all my cousins had to sit at the kids' table.

And now I was officially back—in the fold again. Yet this time something felt different. As I knocked on the front door, my stomach ached with a dull throbbing sensation, similar to how I'd felt after I scarfed too much free clam chowder during break time at Gladstones. But this wasn't a case of excessive butter or cream. It was guilt. So where was it coming from?

Aunt Nannette answered the door in an apron, with her hair swept up and dangly gold earrings hanging halfway down her neck.

"Hello!" she said, kissing my cheek. "I have to go check on the turkey. Sit down." She disappeared into the kitchen.

The cream-colored couches and the Mexican art depictions of *la Virgen* in the living room were exactly as they'd always been.

In the corner was a side table, where framed photos of Nannette's shoot for Mexican *Vogue* and vacations to Cancún were always displayed proudly. There was also a picture from Nannette's wedding, her three sisters wearing matching baby-pink bridesmaid dresses with '80s-style tulle jutting out dramatically from their shoulders. In the center of the table was an old, crinkled photo of Abi as a young woman, alone, with her arms full of children.

While I waited for the rest of the family to arrive, I walked over to the table and ran my fingers along the cool silver frames. The Medellin sisters were in their late fifties and early sixties now, no longer the ingenues in these photos who dominated dance floors in Marina del Rey. Yet even though decades had passed, soon my mom, aunt Elizabeth, and aunt Sofia would arrive and we'd all be in a room together again. So much had changed since the cramped apartment we'd all shared. And so much had stayed the same.

For one thing, my mom and aunts were still praying novenas, and their intentions—money and health—hadn't budged. There was still an air of constant chaos. Someone losing their job, someone newly diagnosed with breast cancer (four women in my family at that point), someone having trouble making ends meet. And I still wanted to fix it all. Yet there was one glaring difference. My life had moved out of survival mode, and theirs hadn't.

That Thanksgiving, my aunt Sofia walked through the door looking more worn-out and overwhelmed than ever, having raised four kids alone while working a string of poverty-wage jobs. Then the phone rang, and it was my aunt Elizabeth, calling to say that she was running late, because she was stranded waiting for the bus somewhere miles away. It was already getting dark outside.

As I grabbed my keys to go pick up my aunt, I felt awful. Wasn't breaking out of a cycle of struggle what I'd set out to do? Shouldn't it feel good to come home a successful woman? If so, why did I feel so conflicted?

When Elizabeth and I made it back to the house a half hour later, everyone slid into their roles, like actors rehearsing a stage play for the millionth time. The four sisters talked over each other constantly—reminiscing about their childhood in Mexico, old boyfriends, and my grandparents. And without fail, at some point my mom would start fiddling with the stereo, filling the living room with the staccato sound of cowbells and bongos—a scene straight out of our apartment on Marine Street.

Always the instigator, my mom began to spin in place as soon as the music started, swirling her hips, as my aunts joined her one by one, their feet in a syncopated rhythm. Quick quick slow, quick quick slow. They danced together like pros, taking turns performing solos as if they were on *Soul Train*. Aunt Nannette, her hands cutting through the air. Aunt Sofia, taking a little longer to warm up but then pivoting her body from side to side when you least expected it. Aunt Elizabeth, reliving her belly-dancing days by swinging her hips in long continuous waves. Charisma and magnetism effortlessly radiated from each of them, as always, and I looked on with the same awe of my childhood. Recording everything on my phone, I hooted "Woooo!" to egg them on and laughed. Yes, I *really* was home now.

I had spent the last two years in Miami, after moving there for a job as an executive at a Spanish-language television network. It was the perfect place to live after four years of putting in the kinds of hours at the White House that had led my doctor to prescribe me megadoses of vitamin D (to combat a severe deficiency from never seeing the sun). It was in Miami that I reached the goal I'd set back when I was waiting tables at Gladstones. I was making six figures, living in an apartment on the twenty-fourth story of a high-rise, with floor-to-ceiling windows that overlooked the ocean. I swam in turquoise water every weekend and drove a silver BMW. It felt like I had finally achieved the kind of financial stability that had evaded me for so long.

When my mom and Monica came to visit, I took them to the private members club I'd joined to spend hot days lounging on striped beach chairs, and treated them to the kinds of elaborate brunch buffets that come with crepe stations and mounds of shrimp on ice. I loved spoiling them, and watching my mom lie back with her eyes closed in the club's steam room. I assumed that all of our lives would be different now. Easier. Yet when I returned home—after living in Boston, Chicago, DC, and Miami—it was undeniable that my life had been the only one that had radically changed.

The pride I had about creating a new life for myself was laced with financial trauma I'd experienced in my childhood. As is sometimes the case for First and Onlys, the chronic stress of scarcity had hardwired my nervous system, and now, being around my family was resurfacing those old wounds. Simply establishing financial autonomy and boundaries felt like I was abandoning them.

When I traveled to other countries on vacation or stayed at nice hotels, I always thought of how much my mom would enjoy being there but would likely never have the chance. When I easily booked an appointment with a specialist and the doctor took the time to answer all of my questions respectfully, I knew that my mom and aunts weren't having the same experience. Doctors often dismissed their pain and minimized their symptoms. Even shopping at Whole Foods felt heavy at times, knowing that I had family members scraping by to afford groceries.

How could I reconcile the guilt I felt for "doing better" than my elders? It was like when I opened the fridge as a child and saw it empty other than one section marked ALI's FOOD. I didn't want to be the only one. What added to this disorienting dynamic was that my family was truly happy for me.

"Send me pictures. I live vicariously through you," my mom often told me with a proud smile on her face.

The sentiment was beautiful, yet I'd always return her smile half-heartedly. I didn't want her to experience things through *me*; I wanted her to experience them for *herself.*

I was in a common in-between land for First and Onlys. Successful enough to breathe easier and start saving some money, yet not successful enough to bring my entire family along with me. I wanted to give the people I loved an easier life. Some First and Onlys have families that even expect it from them.

What makes the pressure feel all the more real is that it's actually possible to buy some degree of happiness for your family. A study by two Nobel laureates in 2010 found that money doesn't buy happiness—unless you make under $75,000 a year. Up until that point, emotional well-being *does* rise with income, because there is trauma in living one paycheck, unseen expense, or illness away from financial ruin. To quote the '90s rock band Everclear, "I hate those people who love to tell you money is the root of all that kills, they have never been poor, they have never had the joy of a welfare Christmas." For First and Onlys, knowing that we technically have the ability to help decrease the emotional pain of our family members can make spending money on ourselves feel selfish.

The growing chasm between my experiences and those

of my family members hadn't been as obvious while I lived on the East Coast, but when I moved back home it was sitting smack in the middle of the table between us, right next to the Thanksgiving turkey. I was overcome with Breakaway Guilt, the gnawing, often lingering, anguish that we sometimes feel about having access to opportunities, experiences, or resources that other people in our families simply do not have. And my Breakaway Guilt didn't only extend to my family.

A week after Thanksgiving, while scrolling through rental listings for lofts in Downtown LA, I switched gears and started googling nonprofits instead. Moving home and regularly driving down Pico Boulevard in Santa Monica was bringing up all sorts of memories: visiting Virginia Park, meeting Spider, and—the earliest fork in my road— writing a play through the Virginia Avenue Project. If I were to think back to the time I needed emotional support the most (and when it would've made the most difference), it was during my teenage years, as I grasped for a way to cope. Back then, I had turned to one-sided relationships and extreme perfectionism, which ultimately only made things worse.

Lately, I'd had an overwhelming desire to spend time with kids who were at that same crossroads. My big homecoming had surfaced flashbacks of how it felt to be their age, and I wanted to give them what I wished I'd had. Mainly, the idea that they didn't have to destroy themselves in order to survive emotional pain—like I almost did. I came across the nonprofit InsideOut Writers, which offers creative writing classes to incarcerated juveniles in LA. Reading about the nonprofit's "healing-informed" work, I knew it was exactly what I was looking for.

Two months later, after being fingerprinted and passing a background check by the Los Angeles County Probation Department, I started substitute teaching inside a juvenile hall in Downtown LA. On the nights I taught, about a dozen twelve- to seventeen-year-old mostly Brown and Black girls were led into my makeshift classroom in a single-file line, wearing head-to-toe gray. I guided them through a range of exercises, from filling out self-esteem worksheets to writing letters to their six-year-old selves and sharing their "rose" and "thorn" from the previous week. Without fail, by the end of class someone would be in tears.

Kendra was a fifteen-year-old third-generation gang member from the South side of LA. When she first showed up to my class, cropped braids on her head and dark-brown eyes fixed on the ground, her arms were always crossed defiantly. I could tell the other girls respected her by the way they glanced at her periodically for approval. When it came time for the girls to go around in a circle and share their writing, I didn't expect Kendra to have written much of anything. She had stared at the wall for most of the hour and had picked up her pen only when I warned her that we had ten minutes left in class. But when it was her turn, Kendra cleared her throat and mumbled a poem that was soulful, raw, and rhythmic.

When she finished, the group sat there for moment of

stunned silence, before erupting into cheers. Kendra shook her head shyly.

"You can keep that," she said, handing me the paper with a smile.

As I tucked it away in my bag, I thought, *This girl is talented.*

At the end of class, I collected each of their pens, counting to make sure I had all of them as I'd been instructed to do each week by the prison guard who escorted me in.

"I hope you'll come back next week, Kendra. You're a really good writer," I told her as a detention guard escorted her out of the room, hands held together behind her back.

I had been just a couple of years younger than Kendra when Leigh at the Virginia Avenue Project first put a pen in my hand—the one that led to my first play and Angela Bassett's encouragement. That pen might as well have been an oar while I was drifting alone at sea; it was that impactful. Now, I had the pens.

Kendra looked back and nodded before walking out.

At the end of each class, I could see the guards securing the girls back into their confined solitary cells, while I was ushered to the dead-bolted exit out of the detention unit. The heavy door would slam shut behind me, leaving me free in the fresh night air and the girls triple-locked inside. And then, without fail, the Breakaway Guilt would hit. By the time I reached the car, my stomach would be churning, imagining the night they had ahead of them while I went home to order takeout.

I was just like them once. Emotionally hardened to survive my circumstances, and only one slipup away from juvenile hall. Why had I been able to dodge going to juvi and they hadn't? Kendra reminded me of myself.

I was struck by how arbitrary and unfair it all seemed, and I didn't want to be yet another person who parachuted in and out of their lives. I had the option of continuing to sub for teachers whenever my schedule allowed, but I wanted to make a real commitment to these girls. So I became a regular teacher for one of the girls housing units and started leading my own weekly writing class. Wednesday nights became sacred on my calendar.

There was something unexpectedly comforting about sharing writing—and a dozen sprinkle doughnuts—with each other every week. For all of us. There may have been a detention guard standing right outside the door, but in my ad hoc classroom, everyone's feelings, thoughts, and words mattered. Little by little, the girls (and guards) warmed to me, and hugs started to replace nods goodbye. The idea that I might do for any of them what the Virginia Avenue Project did for me—introduce a sense of possibility—made our class the highlight of my week.

Two years later, in 2016, I was still teaching my class when Donald Trump was elected president. California's political landscape had to quickly recalibrate from the domino effect of the election cycle: Kamala Harris had won her race for the US Senate, and Xavier Becerra, who represented my LA district in Congress, was appointed to fill her soon-to-be-vacated role as our state's next attorney general, which would then tip off a special election to fill *his* congressional seat. Running for office hadn't been on my radar until I arrived at the Kennedy School, and even then I tucked it away in the who-knows-what-the-future-holds file in my brain. But when I heard Trump call for repealing the Affordable Care Act—a move I knew would impact health-care access for millions—I knew I had to do something.

Most people in my life were unaware that while I was living in Miami, I had taken a hereditary-cancer genetic test at my gynecologist's office on a whim. I was looking for answers after watching so many women in my family develop breast cancer. When the nurse handed me my results in a plain manila envelope—revealing that I carried a BRCA2 gene mutation and had an 85 percent chance of developing breast cancer—I was determined to be proactive.

Yet the only reason I had preventive surgical options to lower my risk was because I had access to good healthcare. And now, millions of people were in jeopardy of having their own options taken away, a move that would particularly impact those with preexisting conditions.

Every day, the news out of Washington was more depressing. And every day, I considered how best to join the fight. The following month, when a special election was called to fill the congressional seat in my district, I recognized that feeling in my gut again. The one I'd followed to Boston and then to DC. It said: *This is how you can help. Run for Congress.* Never mind that it would be the highest Blind-folded Cliff Jump I'd ever attempted.

I quickly learned why running for office is typically a privilege reserved for a select few. There was a reason why only 2 percent of Americans had ever run for office and why the majority of those candidates were white men. Wanting to run for office and being *able* to run for office are two very different things. One reason? Money.

"If you want to demonstrate your viability as a candidate to our organization and to the field at large, you'll need to raise one hundred thousand dollars in ten days," the political director for a well-respected donor network told me. I didn't know how to gauge the feasibility of my run, and I was looking for a metric to help determine my capacity.

"Ten days?" I gasped. To basically raise the equivalent of a college education.

"My advice is to start working the phones immediately," the political director said. "Keep me posted on how you do."

I burned out the battery on my cell phone over the next ten days—eating every meal at my desk, barely sleeping, and calling every person I could think of to ask for a contribution to my campaign. Before each call, I stared at the phone in dread. As someone who had been working to support herself financially since she was in her early teens and who prided herself on her independence, I hated asking people for money. Still, I kept reminding myself why I was doing it, and pushed through.

"This is the friends-and-family round," one of my Kennedy School classmates had said as we talked through my fundraising approach. "Don't worry. I'll bet your family alone will get you most of the way there."

I just looked at him, speechless.

Here I was, raising tens of thousands of dollars each day for a political campaign, and my aunt in her sixties was living in a one-hundred-square-foot studio with no air-conditioning or heat. I didn't know how to explain to my friend that rather than ask my family to donate to my campaign, *I* should be the one helping *them*. There went that Breakaway Guilt again.

On day ten, I was still a few thousand dollars short. Holed up in my apartment, I scrolled through all the contacts on my phone frantically. Who believed in me? Who would stand by my side when I needed them the most? Making donor calls felt like paying a visit to the ghosts of my past lives, *A First Gen Christmas Carol*. There was the close friend and sorority sister from USC who refused to donate because she didn't share my "political beliefs," the Kennedy School classmate who kindly interrupted my spiel to say "Just tell me what you need," and the state senator whose basement I lived in during the Obama campaign who offered to throw me a fundraiser.

As I tried to find someone new to call, I scrolled past the name of a film producer I'd only recently been introduced to by a mutual friend. Normally, I wouldn't feel comfortable even asking him to lunch, but I crossed my fingers in the air and dialed his number anyway. One. Last. Try.

"I'll make a donation of twenty-seven hundred dollars," the producer said over the phone. I mouthed an enthusiastic *Yes!* to myself before responding "Thank you very much" as professionally as possible. With his contribution, I was over the line. I had done it. Raised more than $100,000 in ten days. I was in the race.

Sort of.

I quickly learned that the $100,000 had been only the first of many hoops waiting to be jumped through. I still had to hire a campaign team, build a website, and, of course, make a public announcement.

Thanks to recommendations from friends and old White House colleagues, I quickly hired a small team of staff and political consultants, and we set out to declare my candidacy in the *Los Angeles Times*. Each of the candidates who'd already joined the race had been interviewed for the paper, leading to a short write-up. I threw myself into prep mode with my team—putting together my platform and drafting answers to the typical questions I might be asked.

The day of my announcement interview, I had a pile of notecards in front of me. I had been up late the night before poring over relevant news stories, and I had written out a "statement of purpose" about why I was running. When it came time to speak with the reporter, my communications staff was listening in on a connected line, to ensure that I was ready to address any number of policy questions that she might ask.

The interview started off well, and then there it was.

"I want to ask you about posing in *Maxim*. Do you care to comment on that?"

I gripped the phone tightly and attempted to sound nonchalant.

"I'm not sure what that has to do with my candidacy," I told the reporter. I'd had a feeling this might come up.

"So you have no comment?"

I felt trapped again. If I said anything more to her, I was potentially giving the story new legs. But by not saying anything, I felt stuck where I'd always been—in defensive mode, as if I had done something wrong. I wished I could call out its irrelevance and, at the same time, stand up against sexism in politics. But when I had warned my campaign team earlier that this might happen, we agreed that it was better to not answer any questions about *Maxim*, so I kept silent. I hung up the phone already feeling defeated. Hello again, Impostor Syndrome Plus.

"I cannot believe she asked you that!" gasped my communications consultant when she called me moments later.

"I just hope she doesn't include it in my announcement," I told her.

Later that week, my announcement ran in the paper with no mention of *Maxim*. On our daily team call, everyone was happy that we had dodged a bullet and could now go back to working on the important issues.

Yet it kept coming up. At tea with a female community leader ("The pictures will be a problem, you know") and with a Los Angeles City Council member who was offering well-meaning advice ("Be ready to talk about it at the upcoming debate"). I'd come home to an empty apartment after those conversations and spend the night ruminating that it would never be enough. Everything I'd done, every validator I'd secured. Even after years at the White House, *I'd* never be enough.

One afternoon during my daily call time, my fundraising consultant handed me a spreadsheet she had created from my phone's contact list.

"We're calling through all of these today," she said, sitting across from me in my apartment building's conference room.

The name of a Beverly Hills restaurateur who had been friendly with my mom was at the top of the list. His ego was as big as the chandeliers that lined his restaurant's dining room, and I looked over at my consultant as if to say *Do I have to?*

"You have to call *everyone*," she said, nodding. "Remember why you're doing this."

I sat on hold for ten minutes while his assistant tried to get him on the line, and when he finally picked up, I'd barely shared the news that I was running before he interrupted, telling me how busy he was.

"Meet me at seven tonight in the lobby of the Beverly Hills Hotel for a drink, and we can discuss everything then," he said, hanging up the phone before I had a chance to respond. This was a man used to getting his way.

As I sat in rush hour traffic from Downtown LA to Beverly Hills later that afternoon, I kept reminding myself of my fundraiser's words. *Remember why you are doing this.* I had been through a lot worse; I could surely sit through a drink with an obnoxious man if it meant having more resources to knock on doors.

But when I arrived in the lobby of the hotel, he wasn't there. I walked the entire length of the lobby and looked in the restaurant, but I didn't see him anywhere. Reaching in my purse for my phone, I dialed his number.

"Hi, I'm here. Where are you?" I said, hoping that he was sitting in an area I hadn't checked.

"I'm finishing up a meeting in my room. Meet me here. I'll text you my room number."

Every alarm bell in my head began going off. Wary, I didn't respond.

"I have a suite, so there's a nice living room in here where we can sit and talk. Listen, I need to wrap up a meeting, so just meet me in my room and then we'll go back downstairs to the lobby in a few minutes." Then he hung up abruptly again.

His tone had implied that my hesitation was ridiculous, and I told myself that maybe it was. This was the kind of thing that happened on Hollywood casting couches, not in US House races.

When I walked into the dimly lit room, he was pacing on his cell phone in the middle of a heated conversation, but he waved me over to the couch. We were in a living room with a sitting area, like he'd said, and I felt my shoulders begin to relax a bit. As I took out a folder containing my campaign literature, he motioned for me to pour myself a glass of wine. I grabbed a bottle of water instead.

"Sorry about that. So you want to be a politician, huh?" he said, walking over and sitting right next to me on the couch. He was uncomfortably close, and I scooted back in my seat to create more distance between us.

"Yes. I want to talk to you about my campaign and what I hope to do in Washington. I'd appreciate your support," I said, trying to ignore the intensity behind his eyes.

He looked at me with a self-satisfied grin on his face. "We don't have to waste our time on that," he said. "I will support you, of course."

"You don't know how much that means to me. Thank

you," I told him, pulling out a donor sheet for him to fill out with his credit card information.

"In fact, I can help you in a major way," he continued, placing his hand on my leg.

This can't be happening, I thought. *How do I get out of here and, at the same time, preserve this man's ego so he doesn't punish me for it?*

It was a survival tactic that I'd had to learn over the years, and a dynamic that's unfortunately familiar to many First and Onlys. The less agency you have, the more nonsense and harassment you feel you have to put up with.

"If you and I are together tonight, I will raise you one million dollars. How does that sound? Would that help you win?" As he stared lustfully at me, the strong smell of his musky cologne burned my throat. I tried not to gag.

Pretend you think he's joking, I told myself.

"You're so funny. Stop it!" I said, standing to leave. "I have another meeting to head to. But thank you for taking the time."

I raced down the hall, toward the front of the hotel, trying to outrun my shame and his lingering scent. I knew I hadn't done anything wrong, but I still felt dirty and exposed. Between the reporter's fascination with *Maxim* and the indecent proposal I'd just received, I wanted to throw my hands up and say, *You win. I give up.*

When I got home that night, I was too tired to sleep. I lay in bed, drifting off, but anxious thoughts and my racing heart jolted me awake every few minutes. I had been warned that running for office puts every single aspect of who you are under the lens of the world's most unforgiving microscope. That combined with little sleep (under five hours a night) and not eating well (there were days I ate only a handful of Hershey's Kisses), the pressure would be constant and unbearable. Sleep-deprived and restless, I walked into the bathroom, turned on the light, and looked at my face in the mirror.

Of all the things I'd experienced in my life, what the restaurateur did hadn't been the worst, but like in a game of Jenga, moving one well-placed (emotional) block can knock the whole tower over. Suddenly, something deep inside me broke. Hot tears streamed down my face as I tried to steady myself on the sink, but my legs gave out. I collapsed onto the cold floor, curling into a ball on top of the bath mat. A hoarse cry echoed through my apartment from a voice I didn't recognize as my own. My heart was pumping harder than ever before, yet my entire body felt paralyzed.

This wasn't a panic attack; it was worse. It was the dark hole that had opened up in my chest when Mario threw the ribs at my face, but it was all around me now. Swallowing me. Years of grief and buried pain reaching the surface all at once, as if the stress of the campaign had breached a levee into a well of emotions I'd repressed. *Please, Virgencita…Abi…help me.*

It all came up. What had been building inside me for so long. The parallel wounds of my great-grandmother, my grandmother, and my mom. The attempts I'd made as a child to save everyone else at my own expense. The exasperating ways I tried to compensate for my supposedly incongruent identities. The rush to outpace my lack of belonging. The unacknowledged isolation. The terror I swallowed down along with aspiration and ambition. The eternal outsider status. And the responsibility I still felt to use my life as a mechanism to make my family's sacrifices worth it.

In the process of breaking cycles, forging a new path, and trying to belong, I had done to myself the very thing I was most afraid of. Time and time again—I had held back my feelings, my needs, myself. I had abandoned *myself.* For decades. And for what? To survive? To be liked? To be loved?

I thought I had been doing the work for years to process my feelings and to neutralize my anxiety. Yet, in truth, while I had held my anxiety at bay, I was still living in a constant state of fight or flight. I hadn't done the *deeper* work. I hadn't acknowledged and validated the totality of my own experience. And now the campaign was excavating the evidence of my wounds. I couldn't look away this time.

Rage and sadness poured out of me like an exorcism, and I cried myself into a state of exhaustion. Had it been worth it? And how much more was I willing to give up for external validation if it meant losing myself for good? If I sacrificed any more of myself, there would be nothing left. I'd stomp out my own light once and for all. Staring up at the bathroom ceiling, finally numb and hollow, I drifted off to sleep in the early morning light.

I woke up midmorning, still on the bathroom floor, my temples throbbing. The bathroom light had stayed on all night, and I shielded my stinging eyes with the back of my arm. A script started playing in my head that I knew all too well: *You're fine. Get up. Let it go. Move on.*

As I lay there on my back, I considered shoving everything down as I'd always done and persisting, but I didn't feel like I could do that anymore. In the past, I'd been afraid to stand up for myself, and that had limited my ability to stand up for anyone else. Not anymore. From here on out, I would have the courage to be disliked, and I'd take back my own story. I'd show up. Speak up.

Wiping my face with a towel, I felt around for my phone. Then, pulling myself up from the ground, my legs solid again, I immediately dialed one of my campaign advisors to let him know that I'd decided to write an op-ed.

"Great. About what?" he asked.

"*Maxim.*"

"I don't know if that's a good idea," he said gently. "It's probably best to not say anything more and let it die down." I knew he was feeling protective of me. He was a seasoned pro with years spent working on national campaigns, and his experience dictated caution.

"Look, I've had something to say for almost ten years, and this time, I'm going to say it," I told him. It was time to finally stand up for twenty-four-year-old me.

I used to think that I had to sand down the rough edges of my past, my choices, my appearance, my family, my pain, and my life in general, until they were smooth and comfortable for everyone else. Thankfully, I was done with that now. It had finally sunk in that walking a "perfect line" as a First and Only would forever be playing a game on other people's terms. I had proven everything there was to prove, met every obstacle put in front of me, and I was still being treated like an impostor. It was time to step out of the shadows of my own life and take a different approach. One that took my power back.

My communications consultant suggested we pitch the idea to *Cosmopolitan*, because of their reach, and an editor at the magazine immediately said yes, asking for an eight-hundred-word draft in a matter of days.

It was soon clear just how much I had been holding in; when I sat down to write, the entire op-ed poured out of me in a few hours. What started off as a missive about my own experience with sexism morphed into a manifesto on celebrating complex, multidimensional women and our nonlinear, sometimes contradictory selves.

After I turned in my draft to the editor at *Cosmo* the following week, I found myself wondering if what I'd written would resonate with anyone else. Maybe my story was just that—*my* story. Yet when the op-ed was published online four days later, my social media mentions immediately started blowing up.

Hundreds, and then thousands, of young women were raising their hands saying that they too had experienced similar dynamics in their lives and workplaces. Even Emily Ratajkowski and Olivia Wilde tweeted the op-ed to their millions of followers, with words of solidarity. When the op-ed went viral, I was in awe to see how many women related to an experience I had repeatedly beat myself up about, thinking I was the uniquely flawed one.

It was the same lesson Angela Bassett had taught me when I was in middle school coming back around again: Vulnerability can transform emotional pain into connection.

This time, it really sank in.

As we neared Election Day, the field of candidates ballooned to over twenty people (eighteen Democrats alone). Since many of us held similar positions on the issues, political debates presented rare opportunities to differentiate ourselves from our opponents, and I made a point to participate in every debate I was invited to.

Unfortunately, because there were so many candidates, we each barely had time to answer only one, maybe two, brief questions. In an earlier debate, I sat onstage for two hours and spoke for about two minutes. We weren't exactly getting to the bottom of any issues in the district. Nevertheless, I was eager to make my closing argument to the voters in the final debate before Election Day. Then I saw the date.

Once a year, InsideOut Writers, the nonprofit I was volunteering with, held a writers showcase at the juvenile hall where I taught my class. It was the only opportunity for our students to read their writing to an audience—and for many of them, it would be their first time public speaking, standing on a stage, or using a microphone. The incentive for participation included Subway sandwiches, chips, doughnuts, a DJ, and the chance to feel like a normal kid at a high school talent show, if only for just the afternoon.

As a teacher, my job was to prepare our class to present their poetry, a process that took well over a month. Encouraging the girls not to give up on their writing, helping them to select one of their poems, and then, during the final class before the showcase, rehearsing the run of show with them when their nerves were at their peak.

Since I had been teaching for three years by then, I knew from experience that some girls would be a last-minute flight risk. In the weeks before the showcase, they searched my eyes for reassurance that they weren't going to make fools of themselves. They were uncharacteristically spooked, balling up unfinished poems in frustration and throwing them in the trash.

It made sense that they might be tempted to bail. Their poems were honest and sensitive—exposing stories of abuse, neglect, and heartbreak. And from the stage, their view would be the expressionless faces of hundreds of peers, including gang rivals. Maintaining a reputation of toughness was important to them, both inside Central and back in their neighborhoods, when they eventually got out. I needed to be there for the final class before the showcase to talk them down from quitting on the spot and missing out on an experience that could be potentially transformative. As luck would have it, our dress rehearsal was on the exact same night as the final candidate debate. Less than two weeks before Election Day.

I tried to tell myself that missing the debate wasn't an option. That a substitute teacher could fill in for me and that the girls would be all right. But I knew in my heart that wasn't the case. I mapped out the driving distance between the detention facility and the debate auditorium on my phone, trying to massage the timing just right so that I could speed from one to the other without missing either. It was impossible. If I taught my class that night, I would be over an hour late to the debate.

As I grappled with the possibility of letting the girls

down to maintain my own ambitions, I realized that in reality, it wasn't about choosing between the class and the debate. It was about determining what I truly wanted to do, and then not going against it out of an impulse to people-please or out of guilt or fear. Not looking for approval or validation from anyone other than myself. And once I removed the influence of what I felt I *should* do or what was expected of me, I had no doubt what I wanted to do.

My girls already felt discarded and judged by many of the people in their lives and society at large. Showing up for them was like showing up for myself at thirteen, when I was reeling from the collapse of my mom's marriage and looking for ways to numb myself. I wasn't going to abandon either of us. I would teach my full class and be late for the debate, suffering whatever the consequences might be.

Teaching in juvi and participating in a political debate were worlds apart when it came to mindset and attire, yet I'd need to bolt directly from one to the other without blinking. As a teacher, I was required to dress in logo-less, loose-fitting, casual clothes and shoes, and I generally showed up in a ponytail, without a stitch of makeup. On the night of the debate, I wore my usual shapeless jeans, a plain white T-shirt, and tennis shoes.

After passing through security and several locked chain-link fences on the way to the classroom, I sat with a group of teenage girls as they took turns reciting their innermost thoughts over cheeseburgers (a rare permission I'd cleared with the guards beforehand). One girl, in particular, stood firmly, holding her poem in the air like a scroll.

As she read each word with conviction, I couldn't help but smile. I knew I'd made the right choice.

"Tonight was really great, guys. You all did a wonderful job. Do you feel ready for Saturday?" I asked at the end of class, clearing burger wrappers from the table.

"Yeahs" and nodding heads filled the room. Not one girl backed out.

I'll never know if having the opportunity to voice their otherwise unsaid feelings on a stage had the same effect on them as it had on me when I was their age. But holding a safe space for them to feel what it was like to speak the truth that night was a love letter to the women I knew they (and I) could be.

When I got back to my car, I drove as fast as I could straight to the debate auditorium. Parking far away from any light, I stripped off my street clothes and reached to the back seat, where I had stashed a polished black jumpsuit and three-inch black boots. My mom once told me that the reason she always wore the same shade of intense magenta lipstick was because bright colors make your face look put-together. With not a minute to spare, I smeared scarlet lipstick across my lips, shook my hands through the roots of my hair, and jogged toward the double doors at the entrance.

From the back of the auditorium, I could see my fellow candidates seated in a half circle onstage, microphones on folding tables in front of them. Someone was in the middle of answering a question and had the full attention of an otherwise-silent room. I started to plot out in my head how on earth I'd be able to get onto the stage and over to the one seat left conspicuously open, without creating a total scene. There was no conceivable way. I'd have to walk right up to the front of the room and climb the stairs in full view.

My heels clacked loudly on the wooden floorboards as I went down the center aisle. I could feel the eyes of the audience watching me as I took my seat, now almost an hour and a half late. Hoping to spot a friendly face, I glanced at my fellow candidates sitting erect in their seats, wearing carefully chosen suits and dresses. Many of them were First and Onlys themselves, doing the best they could to juggle their own versions of the Trailblazer Toll.

The moderator, noticing my arrival, looked down at his notes. I could tell the next question would be directed at me.

All these people must be thinking how disrespectful I am, I thought. *Or that I just don't care.*

"Miss Campoverdi, this question is for you," the moderator said, snapping me back into the present moment.

"Thank you. Before I answer your question, though, I want to apologize to everyone for being late tonight and, if I could, I would like to explain the reason why. I teach a writing class to girls incarcerated in juvenile hall, and tonight was a very important night for them. I made a commitment to be there, and I couldn't let them down. I hope you can see my decision as reflective of why I would be the best person to represent you in Congress."

And then I went on to answer his policy-focused question.

The debate ended shortly thereafter, and as the room

started to empty out, I joined the rest of the candidates on the auditorium floor, where members of the community were lingering to ask follow-up questions. While some of the other candidates were surrounded by small groups, I found myself mostly standing alone, no doubt as a result of my lateness.

"Excuse me, ma'am?" a young Latina said as she walked up to me, holding a shy little girl in her arms. The woman had bags under her eyes, and her hair was hastily tossed into an unkempt bun.

"Yes, hi. Good to meet you," I said, holding out my hand to shake hers.

"I just wanted to tell you that you made the right decision."

I scrunched my brow, not sure I was understanding what she meant.

"About the kids…in juvi. You made the right call to be with them," she said. "Have a good night," she added before walking away.

My chest flooded with warmth as I watched her leave. She had no idea how much what she'd said touched me.

I was pretty sure that I didn't win many votes that night; in fact, it was more likely that I lost some. But I had shown up for my girls *and* I had shown up for myself. I was getting a taste of what that felt like, and it felt good.

When I got home late that night, I plopped onto the white leather couch that was a carry-over from my life in Miami and turned on CNN to unwind. I was happy yet exhausted, and all I wanted to do was scroll through my phone mindlessly before bed. Then, I heard a familiar voice:

"This debate isn't about politics; it's personal. For millions of Americans."

I looked up to see my own face, serious and earnest, speaking about the potential repeal of the Affordable Care Act in my first campaign ad, which was airing nationwide. Instantly, I was transported back to filming the spot a few weeks before. Standing in front of a plain white wall at a soundstage in LA. Feeling the bright floodlights on the ceiling warm the top of my head and shoulders. Dabbing the moisture off my upper lip with the back of my hand while thinking to myself, *Come on. You can do this.*

What you couldn't see in the opening frame of the commercial was my mom. Behind me and off to the left, she sat on a high-top stool, clutching a large sepia-toned photograph a little too tightly and waiting for her cue from the director. She had worn a conservative black sweater and the pearl earrings from her wedding day, and even toned down her magenta lipstick to a politically correct mauvy pink. Yet she looked completely self-conscious.

She had come to this country with dreams of being a performer, and she was gifted onstage, but put a video camera in front of her and she'd freeze faster than a tray of paletas. Seeing her obvious discomfort, I had started to feel bad for asking her to be in my campaign ad. It was cold in the room, and she hated the cold. The stool she was sitting on looked rigid and hard. It was probably irritating her fibromyalgia. She was a nervous driver, and I'd made her drive all the way from Inglewood to the Valley. This wasn't her world, it was mine, and I felt guilty for subjecting her to it.

Between takes, I kept looking back at her. Her eyes

were fixed on the photograph in her hands. I saw her wipe the corner of one of her eyes discreetly, hoping that no one would notice and that she wouldn't mess up her carefully applied eye makeup.

In the photograph she was holding, Abi is in her midtwenties with short brown pin-curled hair, dark lipstick, and a 1950s striped A-line dress with puffed short sleeves. She's smiling lovingly, tilting her heart-shaped face toward the baby—my mom—in her arms.

It struck me that right in that instant, my mom was holding my grandmother, who was holding my mom. And as I stood there staring down the pitch-black lens of a video camera, I suddenly felt both of their arms holding me.

I looked down at my own hands, at the baby-blue rosary interlaced between my fingers, off camera—the rosary that Abi had willed herself out of her deathbed to give me—her beautiful, generous spirit tucked into the folds of my life. I had carried the beads (and her) in my hands as I graduated from high school, USC, and Harvard, on my first and last days at the White House, and at every First and Only milestone. Abi was my guardian angel, protecting me. And she was so present now. In my mother's hands, in my hands, in the dialogue of my ad as I talked about the breast cancer that took her life. Her goodness had provided me with an internal compass. She had given me her light.

I looked back at my mom again, sitting there obviously uneasy but showing up for me all the same. Then a flash of gold around her neck caught my eye. It was the medallion of *la Virgen* that my mom had put on when she was pregnant with me, as an offering to ensure my health and safety.

Virgencita, protégenos. She had never stopped wearing it, for almost four decades. Just as she had been imperfectly yet consistently over my shoulder in the background—slightly out of frame—for all of my whims and cliff jumps throughout the years. Calling me her "star" and believing I was destined for something great, because I had been her miracle baby.

I might've not seen her behind me in the past, but lately I had begun to develop an appreciation for just how influential her can-do attitude and resourcefulness had been on my life. "We will always be okay. We'll always figure out a way," she'd said to me when things were especially hard. Her ballsy spirit had egged me on. She had given me her fire.

And then there was my sister Monica, in camouflage pants and Converse high-tops, watching from behind the cameraman. She was now twenty-four years old, but it felt like I'd been carrying her on my hip only minutes ago. I could feel her eyes taking it all in. What I was saying, doing. Our mom, our grandmother. Absorbing, exactly as I had. I hoped that I had set a good example for her. That she felt a sense of possibility and worth.

The truth—my truth—was that I would not be who I was without both of my mothers. Abi—the giver, the helper, the one with unshakable faith. And my mom—the dreamer, the go-getter, the one who always found a way. Yes, I was technically disrupting their cycles as a First and Only, but at the end of the day, I was actually integrating them. Like the pigtail braids my mom used to weave into my hair as a child or the song she says reminds her of us—Mon Laferte's "La Trenza." Abi and my mom still moved through me continuously, not as patterns that needed to be discarded or forgotten, but as the evolution of our family's story, rebuilt and renewed. The understanding that we were all in this together helped to counterbalance my lingering Breakaway Guilt. The idea that we can be our ancestors' living memorial.

It was all three of us filming that day—together as we once had been in my grandmother's womb, when Abi carried my mom, whose ovary contained the egg that would become me. Passing blessings between us like the crosses we had always drawn on each other's foreheads. Over three generations, we had been connected in so many ways known and unknown, the most recent being that as I sat there on the couch watching my campaign ad, an undetected cancer was forming in one of my breasts. I would be diagnosed the following year, becoming the fourth generation of women in my family to have the disease. And by far the youngest.

Sitting on the couch that night, I thought of how my life might drastically change—once again—if I were to be elected to Congress. Going to Washington during such a divisive time would test me in every way, and I'd no doubt be facing the same headwinds of sexism and underestimation as before. Yet the fact that I was in contention at all felt like something worth reflecting on. I had just watched my campaign ad run on CNN. I had raised hundreds of thousands of dollars in less than four months. I had knocked on doors, debated my opponents, and met with community leaders. In a hilarious twist, even *Maxim* had issued a public endorsement of my candidacy. Win or lose—I was in the arena.

When I was a waitress at Gladstones—before graduate school ever entered my mind—a businessman with a chiseled square jaw came in for lunch alone one day. As he followed the hostess through the restaurant, his black suit standing out among the fanny-pack-wearing tourists, I thought, *Come on. Be seated in my section.* And he was. I couldn't believe my luck.

As I walked over to take his order, he smiled at me, dimples popping, and my stomach did a backflip. I filled his glass with water, regretting that I hadn't done more with my hair than toss it into a sloppy ponytail. After he ordered a sandwich and iced tea, we made small talk and he shared that he was in town for work.

"Right now, I work internationally in business, but my goal is to one day be a US senator," he told me, with the kind of self-assurance that I wished I had. From where I stood, it seemed so possible for him. He mentioned he'd gone to an Ivy League school, and he was wearing leather loafers in the Malibu sun.

When he left and I picked up his check from the table, he had left not only a generous tip, but also his business card with his cell phone number scribbled on the back.

I want to be a senator's wife, I said to myself, folding the card into my back pocket. I wanted to be at the side of someone who would change the world for the better. We exchanged a few messages in the months that followed, but we never saw each other again.

Back then, being a politician's wife was as close to politics as I could imagine myself. And now, here I was legitimately in contention to be a member of Congress. I was filled with an unexpected sense of calm, realizing that everything I'd been through had mattered. The lessons, the muscle memory, the scars, all of it. I wondered if that businessman ever ran for office and how he'd react to learning that I had. The woman who wiped up his ketchup.

I turned off the television and walked into the bathroom to brush my teeth. Staring at my face in the mirror again, this time I felt peace. I realized that while Election Day would be monumental, it didn't take precedence over everything else that I'd seen, experienced, and built. The way I'd started to come home to myself and stand up for myself.

My First and Onlys—the Election Days, graduations, and awards—had gotten all the top billing, but those days had made up only about 5 percent of my life. The other 95 percent was who I was. I had been in a race against time to cycle-break/achieve/prove for the better part of my life. Now, at thirty-seven years old, I decided that no matter what happened at the polls, I would choose to spend the rest of my life savoring the other 95 percent. I'd give myself permission to focus on joy and peace.

My climb as a First and Only was, in many ways, a mad dash toward belonging. What I was willing to sacrifice for it. Trade for it. Abandon for it. How I twisted and silenced myself to fit into the different versions of me that I wore like ill-fitting costumes. We all want to be accepted; we all want to belong. But for many years, I didn't grasp that as long as I kept losing myself in the process, it and I would never be enough. I might possess all the external trappings of the American Dream, but I'd never grasp the sense of wholeness I'd been searching for all my life.

The vital piece I was missing was the acknowledgment and naming of my own emotional scar tissue. Not because I had a chip on my shoulder or because I needed someone to blame, but because our greatest power is in being fully known to ourselves. It's how we know where we still need healing, so that when we meet our goals, we are able to receive their gifts with a balanced heart, mind, and body. It's how we learn to celebrate who we are versus what we've accomplished.

There will probably always be a part of me that is conditioned to track my belonging in the spaces I inhabit, just like I'll probably always be someone who leans to the anxious side and feels a degree of Breakaway Guilt, but when I ultimately allowed myself to let go of the driving need to Belong (with a capital *B*), I realized that I always had.

To a lineage of women who had the audacity to exist in places that hadn't traditionally accepted them. To a community of First and Onlys whose presence in and of itself is a radical act. And most importantly, to myself. It was enough.

The race, the Dream, and the résumé were never the point. My story—our story as First and Onlys—has never been about *arriving* at any given place. In fact, this story ends in my bathroom on the eve of an election I would go on to lose.

I promised I'd keep it real with you, and this is about as real as it gets: When it comes to borders—whether they're family patterns, social classes, or actual walls—the destination is secondary.

The honor lies in the *crossing*.

IT'S ONLY LOVE THAT GETS YOU THROUGH

RESURFACING THE MEMORIES in this book was like burying my hands in the stones at the bottom of a fishbowl
and then shaking them back and forth. All the shit came
up. Sometimes, quietly—in cathartic tears as I reread sections to myself or opened an old box of photographs. And
other times, explosively—in clashes with my mom over
our conflicting memories or sleepless nights spent trying
to patch up a wound I'd reopened. To ground myself, I
placed a *veladora de la Virgen* on my desk and lit it whenever I sat down to write. Her company helped. As did surrounding myself with some of the photos I've included in
this book.

Over the last few years, I've devoted a lot of time to
processing the emotional tolls and family dynamics associated with being a First and Only—books, webinars, energy
healing—yet I continue to be reminded that while our
minds may understand the root of our traumas and want

to move on, our bodies have much longer memories. They want to protect us. So they get triggered and react in ways we swore we had grown past; they search for closure or remorse we swore we didn't need anymore. If you're anything like me, it can feel pretty demoralizing to catch yourself in an old familiar loop.

"I still bow my head," my mom admitted recently as we lingered on the phone, after an emotional fact-checking call turned confessional.

She shared that during their bleakest years in Mexico—when Abi had six kids under the age of twelve and Abito was always on the road—they had no hot water in their home, a one-room concrete block that regularly had *babosos* (slimy black slugs) creeping up its walls. Abi would bathe my mom in a plastic tub with a bucket, having her bow her head forward like she was in church, as she poured water that had been warmed in a pot on the stove onto the crown of her head.

"You know, even now when I'm in the shower, sometimes I catch myself still bowing my head," my mom told me.

I understood where she was coming from. These days, I also find it frustrating when my own head (figuratively) bows, in its own conditioned ways.

I no longer live in a state of fight or flight, but the Trailblazer Toll and the eight components I've touched on—Invisible Inheritances, the Parentified Child, the Bicultural Balancing Act, Chutes and Social Ladders, the Lonely Hustle, Blindfolded Cliff Jumping, Impostor Syndrome Plus, and Breakaway Guilt—remain woven into the fabric of my life. Over the years and along the way, I've gathered knowledge and healing tools, many of which I've referenced in this book. I'm certainly no therapist, trained authority, or trauma expert—and I surely don't have it all figured out—but I share these resources with you here in the hope that one or all of them may ring true for you and be a companion on your journey.

First, I'm including a blank three-generation genogram template. I encourage you to fill one out for your family, despite how much you think you already know about your own Invisible Inheritances. Asking our loved ones to elaborate on family dynamics can bring about difficult conversations but also eye-opening insight. I've also included a key with common emotional relationship symbols, but genograms are meant to be customizable, so feel free to create your own symbols and personalize however makes sense.

The ten-question test for adverse childhood experiences (ACEs) that I mentioned in chapter three is easy to find online and I'm also including a link below. I didn't consider the physical and emotional effects of childhood experiences for a long time, before understanding their proven connection to our health and well-being. Yet the reality is that more than 60 percent of us experience some form of significant trauma as children, with nearly one in six of us experiencing four or more different types of ACEs, and this toxic stress has consequences. Repressed emotions can actually make you sick. The good news is that our ACE score is only one part of the equation, and there are health strategies and mindfulness techniques that can reverse and repair the impact of ACEs. Finding out my own score was revealing but also actionable. Take a moment to learn yours:

- Take the ACE Quiz—And Learn What It Does and Doesn't Mean
    ○ npr.org/sections/health-shots/2015 /03/02/387007941/take-the-ace-quiz -and-learn-what-it-does-and-doesnt-mean

- Healing and Prevention Resources
    ○ numberstory.org/heal-myself/

Next, here is a list of additional resources I've found to be incredibly valuable:

- Self-Reparenting Work
    ○ "Reparenting in Therapy" https://www.verywellmind.com/ reparenting-in-therapy-5226096

- Somatic Therapy
    ○ "What Is Somatic Therapy?" verywellmind.com/ what-is-somatic-therapy-5190064

- Transcendental Meditation
    ○ Center for Resilience davidlynchfoundation.org

- For Anxiety
  - o Cognitive Behavioral Therapy
    "What Is Cognitive Behavioral Therapy
    (CBT)?"
    verywellmind.com/what-is-
    cognitive-behavior-therapy-2795747
  - o Exposure Therapy
    "What Is Exposure Therapy?"
    verywellmind.com/exposure-therapy-
    definition-techniques-and-efficacy-5190514
  - o Book: *Panic Free: Eliminate Anxiety/Panic
    Attacks Without Drugs and Take Control of
    Your Life* by Lynne Freeman, PhD

- Culturally Competent Therapists for POC
  - o Latinx Therapy: latinxtherapy.com
  - o Therapy for Black Girls:
    therapyforblackgirls.com
  - o Boris Lawrence Henson Foundation:
    borislhensonfoundation.org
  - o Inclusive Therapists:
    inclusivetherapists.com
  - o National Queer & Trans Therapists of
    Color Network: nqttcn.com

Finally, a vital part of my own journey has been to make wellness and healing a priority, as well as to be more intentional about where and with whom I choose to invest my emotional energy. For me, it's a daily practice of choosing peace, again and again. Choosing to rest, spend time in nature, practice mindfulness and prayer, guard my energy, take walks, listen to my body, trust my intuition, let go of unhealthy relationships, and, most importantly, give myself grace. To not try to be a "healing perfectionist" and, instead, to allow myself space to be human.

There's no doubt that confronting emotions that have been bottled up inside of us, sometimes for decades, can feel destabilizing. Not to mention that doing this work may compel our loved ones to confront their *own* pain, usually unwillingly, which can sometimes lead to resistance and even conflict. It's okay to feel sad about the lack of understanding and support we sometimes feel from our families about our attempts to heal. Revisiting memories can be daunting and uncomfortable, and there have been times when I wondered if leaving the lid on such an old box might be the smartest choice for all. If I should simply accept the hand I've been dealt and the stories I've told myself about who I am and what I am capable of.

In the end, it was Abi who showed me an alternative.

It was Christmas morning 1985, when I was six years old and an avid Care Bears fan. In a photo taken on that day, I'm standing in the foreground with my arms at my sides, wearing a gray sweatshirt dress with red trim and white lambs on its skirt. There's a ragged-looking Christmas tree behind me to the right, decorated with mismatched ornaments, representing both sides of the US–Mexico border. It's obvious by my posture that I had been directed to "stand in front of the tree" just seconds before. But my face is soft, with a hint of a smile detectable across my lips. I remember the feeling I had in that moment as if it were yesterday: complete and unconditional love.

Behind me to the left is the reason why. A life-sized handmade fireplace sits next to the window, extending across the wall behind our Christmas tree. It's made entirely out of cardboard, down to its pretend bricks, some of which have been darkened with "soot" to be realistic. Fluffy silver tinsel lines the mantel, where my red, white, and green stocking has been hung with care. And cherry-red flames, fashioned out of crinkled aluminum foil, roar out of its hearth into our modest living room.

At that time, I had never seen a fireplace in real life. They existed only in the black-and-white Shirley Temple movies Abi and I watched on the nights my mom went out. But those on-screen fireplaces represented a whole new world to me. Every woman I saw near one wore a silky dress and had shiny hair. Every man who leaned on its mantel wore a tailored suit and held a martini glass. I knew fireplaces belonged in houses with tall chimneys and big grassy yards. Families with both mothers and fathers gathered in front of them to open Christmas presents with their children. As far as I was concerned, a fireplace was a prerequisite for the kind of life I wanted.

Abi saw me. She saw the part of me that couldn't yet articulate what I dreamed of but needed the tools to get there all the same. Which is why on Christmas Eve, she stayed up late building me an elaborate fireplace out of cardboard and foil. I'll never forget running into the living room to see what Santa had left and stopping in my tracks. Abi stood off to the side watching as I slowly walked up to the fireplace, instinctively holding out my hands to feel the warmth of its flames on my skin. I couldn't believe it. She had taken my deepest wish and willed it into reality.

I learned something critical that day that has been a lifeline throughout my healing journey as a First and Only. Sometimes, despite all the striving or the knowledge we gain, despite our accolades or the partners we have, despite the boundaries we set with our families or how successful we are at rescuing everyone else, security and serenity may still feel like goalposts that keep moving.

Healing work requires us to unnumb ourselves, and it often feels worse before it gets better. But turning to positivity at the expense of our own emotional truth is never the solution. As Abi demonstrated, we're more powerful than we give ourselves credit for. Everything we need to be okay is already inside of us. Radiating from the innermost part of us. There is nothing we've been searching outside of ourselves for that we can't just as easily create. Especially our own peace and healing.

We can be the ones to build it—and to keep rebuilding over and over again—each time it gets knocked down.

With our own hands. Out of cardboard if necessary.

THE JOURNEY

One day you finally knew
what you had to do, and began,
though the voices around you
kept shouting
their bad advice—
though the whole house
began to tremble
and you felt the old tug
at your ankles.
"Mend my life!"
each voice cried.
But you didn't stop.
You knew what you had to do,
though the wind pried
with its stiff fingers
at the very foundations—
though their melancholy
was terrible.
It was already late
enough, and a wild night,
and the road full of fallen
branches and stones.
But little by little,
as you left their voices behind,

the stars began to burn
through the sheets of clouds,
and there was a new voice,
which you slowly
recognized as your own,
that kept you company
as you strode deeper and deeper
into the world,
determined to do
the only thing you could do—
determined to save
the only life you could save.

—Mary Oliver

*Credit: "The Journey" from Dream Work by Mary Oliver. Copyright © 1986 by Mary
Oliver. Used by permission of Grove/Atlantic, Inc.*

FIRST GEN ON *SPOTIFY*

bit.ly/firstgenplaylist

"Fast Car"
Tracy Chapman

"Born on the Bayou"
Creedence Clearwater Revival

"Amor Eterno"
Juan Gabriel

"Keep Their Heads Ringin'"
Dr. Dre

"Crash Into Me"
Dave Matthews Band

"On the Bound"
Fiona Apple

"How to Save a Life"
The Fray

"Everlong"
Foo Fighters

"La Trenza"
Mon Laferte

"It's Only Love That Gets You Through"
Sade

Genogram

Great-Grandparents

Grandparents

Parents

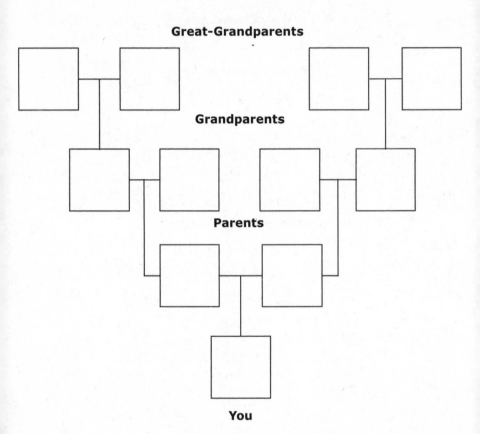

You

Genogram Emotional Relationship Symbols

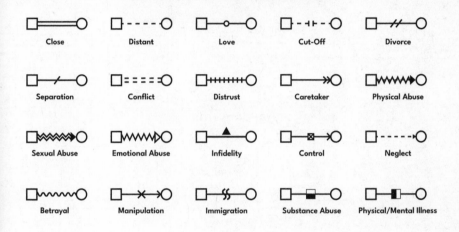

Close	Distant	Love	Cut-Off	Divorce
Separation	Conflict	Distrust	Caretaker	Physical Abuse
Sexual Abuse	Emotional Abuse	Infidelity	Control	Neglect
Betrayal	Manipulation	Immigration	Substance Abuse	Physical/Mental Illness

ACKNOWLEDGMENTS

To Abi and Abito, and all of my ancestors who whispered in my ear throughout the writing of this book. I celebrate you.

To my mom, Cecilia, whose stories were told in the telling of my own. Not once did you ask me to hold anything back. For that, I am eternally grateful. Thank you for your bravery, for sharing your memories, and for loving me so much. I love you with all my heart.

My sister Monica, you'll forever be my baby. Thank you for your unwavering faith and support, and for taking me to the wildflowers that day. I'm so proud of who you've become. Mario Uribe, my great-uncle, for being so generous with your memories of Abi and of your mother, Maria Elena. I appreciate you. Aunts Nannette, Elizabeth, and Sofia, I'm always thinking of you.

To 11, my first reader and biggest cheerleader, for challenging me to live these words. Leigh Curran, for using your gifts to change so many lives, mine included. Dr.

ACKNOWLEDGMENTS

Lynne Freeman, this book might've ended in chapter five if it weren't for you. Dominique Sire, my healing journey would not be the same without your guidance and transformative work.

And to the people without whom this book would not exist: my wonderful editor, Karyn Marcus, for your trust and care, and for bringing this book to life. I'm deeply grateful to you. Everyone at Grand Central (Hachette) who worked to edit, review, design, typeset, champion, and promote this book, and to Elizabeth Johnson for her extraordinary attention to detail, and to Ian Dorset, Roxanne Jones, Alana Spendley, and Zohal Karimy. My extraordinary agents, Andy McNicol and Liz Parker, and the team at Verve. For believing from day one and for walking by my side every step of the way. Christine Pride, I simply cannot thank you enough for your support and encouragement.

Special thank-yous to: Chrysta Bilton, Bob Roth, Tamara Klajn, Mike de la Rocha, Mona Sutphen, Marjorie Blum, Jimmy Wu, Rimjhim Dey, Andy DeSio, and Jessica Zagacki. To all of my extended friends and family who sent words of encouragement along the way.

And to everyone whose lives and lessons touched these pages, thank you. I would not change a thing.

ABOUT THE AUTHOR

ALEJANDRA CAMPOVERDI is a nationally recognized women's health advocate, founder, producer, and former White House aide to President Obama. She produced and appeared in the groundbreaking PBS documentary *Inheritance*, created *Latinos & BRCA* in partnership with Penn Medicine's Basser Center, and served as the first White House deputy director of Hispanic media. Alejandra is on the boards of Harvard's Shorenstein Center on Media, Politics, and Public Policy, the Friends of the National Museum of the American Latino, and the California Community Foundation, and previously served on the Medical Board of California, as well as the First 5 California Commission. Alejandra holds a Master in Public Policy degree from Harvard's Kennedy School of Government and graduated cum laude from the Annenberg School at the University of Southern California.